DATE DUE

PROBLEM ANALYSIS
RESPONDING TO
SCHOOL COMPLEXITY

Charles M. Achilles

John S. Reynolds

Susan H. Achilles

EYE ON EDUCATION

6 DEPOT WAY WEST, SUITE 106

LARCHMONT, NY 10538

(914) 833–0551

(914) 833–0761 fax

For information about permission to reproduce selections from this book, write: Eye On Education, Permissions Dept., Suite 106, 6 Depot Way West, Larchmont, NY 10538.

ISBN 1-883001-36-6

Library of Congress Cataloging-in-Publication Data

Achilles, Charles M.
    Problem analysis : responding to school complexity / by Charles M. Achilles, John S. Reynolds, Susan G. Achilles
        p.   cm.
    Includes bibliographical references (p.).
    ISBN 1-883001-36-6
        1. School management and organization—United States—Decision-making. 2. School principals—United States. 3. Problem solving. I. Reynolds, John S., 1931–   . II. Achilles, Susan G., 1950–   . III. Title.
    LB2806.A25   19977
    371.2'012—dc21   97-18980
                                                          CIP

10 9 8 7 6 5 4 3

Editorial and production services provided by
Richard H. Adin Freelance Editorial Services
9 Orchard Drive, Gardiner, NY 12525
(914-883-5884)

THE SCHOOL LEADERSHIP LIBRARY

INFORMATION COLLECTION
By Paula Short, Rick Jay Short, and Kenneth Brinson, Jr.

INSTRUCTION AND THE LEARNING ENVIRONMENT
by James W. Keefe and John M. Jenkins

INTERPERSONAL SENSITIVITY
by John R. Hoyle and Harry M. Crenshaw

JUDGMENT: MAKING THE RIGHT CALLS
By Jim Sweeney and Diana Bourisaw

**LEADERSHIP: A RELEVANT AND REALISTIC ROLE
FOR PRINCIPALS**
by Gary M. Crow, L. Joseph Matthews, and Lloyd E. McCleary

MOTIVATING OTHERS: CREATING THE CONDITIONS
by David P. Thompson

ORAL AND NONVERBAL EXPRESSION
by Ivan Muse

**ORGANIZATIONAL OVERSIGHT:
PLANNING AND SCHEDULING FOR EFFECTIVENESS**
by David A. Erlandson, Peggy L. Stark, and Sharon M. Ward

**PROBLEM ANALYSIS:
RESPONDING TO SCHOOL COMPLEXITY**
By Charles M. Achilles, John S. Reynolds, and Susan H. Achilles

RESOURCE ALLOCATION
by M. Scott Norton and Larry K. Kelly

STUDENT GUIDANCE AND DEVELOPMENT
By Mary Ann Ward and Dode Worsham

WRITTEN EXPRESSION: THE PRINCIPAL'S SURVIVAL GUIDE
By India Podsen, Glenn Pethel, and John Waide

If you would like information about how to become a member of the School Leadership Library, please contact:

Eye On Education
6 Depot Way, Suite 106
Larchmont, NY 10538
Phone: (914) 833–0551 Fax: (914) 833–0761

Also Published by Eye On Education

ADMINISTRATOR'S GUIDE TO
SCHOOL-COMMUNITY RELATIONS
by George E. Pawlas

BLOCK SCHEDULING:
A CATALYST FOR CHANGE IN HIGH SCHOOLS
by Robert Lynn Canady and Michael D. Rettig

THE DIRECTORY OF INNOVATIONS IN
ELEMENTARY SCHOOLS
by Jane McCarthy and Suzanne Still

EDUCATIONAL TECHNOLOGY:
BEST PRACTICES FROM AMERICA'S SCHOOLS
by William C. Bozeman and Donna J. Baumbach

THE EDUCATOR'S BRIEF GUIDE TO COMPUTERS IN
THE SCHOOLS
by Eugene F. Provenzo, Jr.

HANDS-ON LEADERSHIP TOOLS FOR PRINCIPALS
by Raymond Calabrese, Gary Short, and Sally Zepeda

LEADERSHIP THROUGH COLLABORATION:
ALTERNATIVES TO THE HIERARCHY
by Michael Koehler and Jeanne C. Baxter

THE PRINCIPAL AS STEWARD
by Jack McCall

THE PRINCIPAL'S EDGE
by Jack McCall

RESEARCH ON EDUCATIONAL INNOVATIONS,
Second Edition
by Arthur K. Ellis and Jeffrey T. Fouts

RESEARCH ON SCHOOL RESTRUCTURING
by Arthur K. Ellis and Jeffrey T. Fouts

THE SCHOOL PORTFOLIO:
A COMPREHENSIVE FRAMEWORK FOR SCHOOL
IMPROVEMENT
by Victoria L. Bernhardt

SCHOOL-TO-WORK
by Arnold H. Packer and Marion W. Pines

TEACHING IN THE BLOCK:
STRATEGIES FOR ENGAGING ACTIVE LEARNERS
Edited by Robert Lynn Canady and Michael D. Rettig

FOREWORD

The School Leadership Library was designed to show practicing and aspiring principals what they should know and be able to do to be effective leaders of their schools. The books in this series were written to answer the question, "How can we improve our schools by improving the effectiveness of our principals?"

Success in the principalship, like in other professions, requires mastery of a knowledge and skills base. One of the goals of the National Policy Board for Educational Administration (sponsored by NAESP, NASSP, AASA, ASCD, NCPEA, UCEA, and other professional organizations) was to define and organize that knowledge and skill base. The result of our efforts was the development of a set of 21 "domains," building blocks representing the core understanding and capabilities required of successful principals.

The 21 domains of knowledge and skills are organized under four broad areas: Functional, Programmatic, Interpersonal, and Contextual. They are as follows:

FUNCTIONAL DOMAINS

Leadership
Information Collection
Problem Analysis
Judgment
Organizational Oversight
Implementation
Delegation

PROGRAMMATIC DOMAINS

Instruction and the Learning
  Environment
Curriculum Design
Student Guidance and
  Development
Staff Development
Measurement and Evaluation
Resource Allocation

INTERPERSONAL DOMAINS

Motivating Others
Interpersonal Sensitivity
Oral and Nonverbal Expression
Written Expression

CONTEXTUAL DOMAINS

Philosophical and Cultural
  Values
Legal and Regulatory
  Applications
Policy and Political Influences
Public Relations

These domains are not discrete, separate entities. Rather, they evolved only for the purpose of providing manageable descriptions of essential content and practice so as to better understand the entire complex role of the principalship. Because human behavior comes in "bunches" rather than neat packages, they are also overlapping pieces of a complex puzzle. Consider the domains as converging streams of behavior that spill over one another's banks but that all contribute to the total reservoir of knowledge and skills required of today's principals.

The School Leadership Library was established by General Editors David Erlandson and Al Wilson to provide a broad examination of the content and skills in all of the domains. The authors of each volume in this series offer concrete and realistic illustrations and examples, along with reflective exercises. You will find their work to be of exceptional merit, illustrating with insight the depth and interconnectedness of the domains. This series provides the fullest, most contemporary, and most useful information available for the preparation and professional development of principals.

Scott Thomson
Executive Secretary
National Policy Board for
   Educational Administration

PREFACE

Schools are complex places, experienced by almost everyone and understood by almost no one. They are cherished in memory, trusted with the future, and blamed for the present. They are shaped by the conflicting demands of professionals, the public, and parents. In many communities across America, they are the largest single employer. They almost always have either too many or too few students to be both efficient and effective. They are in the business of building individual potential by means of a bureaucratic structure. For decades they have been plagued by a wide range of smaller and greater problems—ranging from chewing gum to gang violence, from losing football seasons to intractable reading failure, from disinterested parents to hostile critics. Yet somehow they have continued to survive, stumbling from one problem to another.

A.A. Milne's immortal children's classic, *Winnie the Pooh*, begins with Pooh Bear coming down the stairs behind Christopher Robin, the back of his head bumping on each successive step until he reaches the bottom. He suspects there may be a better way to come down the stairs, but his head never stops bumping long enough for him to figure out what it is. He also suspects that there may not be a better way. Surrounded by constant problems of varying intensity and impact, many principals respond in the same way as Pooh.

The authors of this volume, *Problem Analysis: Responding to School Complexity*, invite the principal to pause and see if there might not be a better way of responding to the barrage of school problems that often promise to destroy any opportunity for thought and reflection. In effect, the authors invite principals to step out of their strait jackets—of bureaucratic thinking, of rules and regulations, of the conventional wisdom—and dream and create. They encourage the principal to use the full range of his or her abilities to actively, find, describe, solve, and reflect on problems.

Charles Achilles, John Reynolds, and Susan Achilles begin with an exposition of what they mean by "problems" and "problem analysis," what these terms mean in relation to the daily operation of the school, and why they are critical to the success of the principal. After presenting this conceptual material they demonstrate what is meant by "problem finding" and "problem solving" and the relationship between them. As their presentation unfolds, cases and vignettes are added to illustrate the concepts they have presented and to assist principals in applying these concepts to the range of problems they face daily in their schools.

If all this sounds too abstract for the reader, we would note that the Problem Analysis dimension of the NASSP Assessment Center has consistently proven to be the most powerful assessment center indicator of a principal's success on the job. The material presented in this book is conceptual, but it is also very practical. Principals who habitually seek to define, solve, and reflect on the problems of the school are very likely to be effective principals. We encourage the principal to loosen up, to draw back from daily pressures, to revisualize the school's problems, and to practice reframing those problems that are keeping him or her awake at night. This book provides an excellent guide for that creative activity.

David A. Erlandson
Alfred P. Wilson

DEDICATIONS

Working on this book caused me to consider how time influences one person's perception of another person's problems. I dedicate my portion of this book to three generations of women in my life whose past and future problems play and replay in my present.

> T.A.A. whose problems I'm only now starting to under stand as I encounter them at her same age but later. Thanks, Mom.

> P.A.A. whose problems I still don't understand, but whose stark and lonely solution was clear. You are missed.

> C.A.A. whose problems I surely could solve if she'd let me, but who prefers to pitch headlong into familiar pits. Problems are growth, daughter.

C.M. Achilles
Geneva, NY 1996

This work is dedicated to my wife Sheila whose love and support make problem analysis and decision making a collaboration and a joy.

J.S. Reynolds
Rock Hill, SC 1996

To CMA: Please remember that no one can understand or solve all of life's problems. Indeed, if problems do provide personal growth, then perhaps they also lead us to new solutions, new people, and new beginnings. *PAX ~ SP ~*

S.H. Achilles
Greenville, SC 1996

ACKNOWLEDGMENTS

Our debt to many people is obvious. We have carefully tried to cite important references throughout and to give appropriate credits. In spite of that, some ideas have been discussed in professional meetings or conference sessions, and we may have lost the exact citations to these. Should we have inadvertent omissions, let us know so that we can make adjustments.

Much work in problem analysis is from fields other than education; few people have explained problem analysis in education. Leithwood and associates have done considerable work on expert problem solving in education. Professor Getzels has written heuristically on problem finding. We have borrowed his terminology for two chapters: "The Problem of the Problem" and "The Problem of the Solution." Paula Silver explored problems of practice in her work at APEX (Advancing Principal EXcellence Center) at the University of Illinois. Appendix A contains an adaptation of some of her early work. Osterman and others extended this agenda for a few years at the Silver Center at Hofstra University. Recently, Bridges and Hallinger (1993) have moved problem-based learning (PBL) from physician preparation into preparation processes for education administrators. We have borrowed unabashedly when such borrowing has aided the idea of problem analysis.

We thank those who have helped us. In spite of their efforts, any deficiencies are the authors' own. David Erlandson cajoled, chided, and corrected. Doctoral students at Eastern Michigan University contributed in a "Problem-finding Seminar." Lloyd DuVall invited one author to present a paper on problem finding at Nova Southeastern University (NSU). Joanna Warder typed, edited, formatted, and asked important questions. Linda Ward provided helpful information about Myers-Briggs' personality/leadership types. Also helping with the case study and vignette development were graduate students from Winthrop University who furnished actual experiences from their administrative routines. Examples have been modified from practicum problems discussed by NSU students. Sheila Reynolds, Jane Zukin, and Jacqueline Davis-Green added editing and helpful ideas. Thank you all.

ABOUT THE AUTHORS

Charles M. Achilles is a generalist who has researched school-related issues, including desegregation, effective schools, public confidence, regionalism, preparation of administrators, and class-size effects on pupil outcomes in primary grades. He is the coauthor of five recent books: *Finding Funding; Grantwriting, Fundraising, and Partnerships; Handbook on Gangs in Schools; Let's Make a Deal;* and *Let's Put Kids First, Finally.*

Currently a professor of Educational Leadership at Eastern Michigan University, he was professor and department chair at the University of North Carolina at Greensboro. He worked more than 20 years in Educational Administration and at the Bureau of Educational Research and Services at the University of Tennessee, Knoxville. He served at the (former) U.S. Office of Education and as a researcher at the University of California, Berkeley after teaching in public and private schools. As a lecturer for Nova Southeastern University, he meets educators who are on the "front lines." From them he learns constantly about problems encountered in America's schools.

Achilles holds an A.B. in classics, M.A. in education and Latin, and an Ed.S. and an Ed.D. in educational administration, all from the University of Rochester, New York.

Susan Hoover Achilles has taught high school English and yearbook production, served as a K–12 gifted and talented education coordinator, and directed an alternative program for at-risk students. Since 1985 she has been both a middle and high school principal in Greenville, South Carolina, where she also serves on the Board of Directors of the Upstate Mediation Network, Piedmont Residential Homes Placement, and South Carolina Children's Advisory Committee. As principal she initiated FANS (*F*amilies *A*nd *N*eighborhood *S*chools) at Bryson Middle School and the SMART Team (*S*tudents *M*aking *A*lternative *R*esolutions *T*ogether), a school-community initiative, at Woodmont High School, one of South Carolina's first sanctioned peer mediation conflict resolution programs. She currently serves as Director of Safe and Drug Free Schools for the District.

Achilles received her B.S. in English from Appalachian State University, M.A. in administration from Furman University, and her Ed.D. in educational leadership from Nova Southeastern University in Fort Lauderdale, Florida.

John S. Reynolds is a professor and program coordinator for the Educational Administration and Supervision Program at Winthrop University in Rock Hill, South Carolina. John has been a teacher, coach, high school principal, superintendent, associate dean, and professor in the field of education. He has been instrumental in establishing field-based graduate administrator programs and he frequently works in local schools to maintain contact with practitioners' concerns. He is an assessor with the South Carolina NASSP Assessment Center.

John was also a city mayor in Florida and has written articles and served as a consultant in the United States and Europe in his areas of specialty—problem solving, human relations, and organizational development. John and his wife Sheila reside in Fort Mill, South Carolina.

Reynolds received his B.A. from Akron State University, M.A. from Appalachian State University, and his Ed.D. from the University of Tennessee, Knoxville.

TABLE OF CONTENTS

1

PROBLEM OR OPPORTUNITY?

This book has five parts. This chapter contains an introduction to and some general information about two main divisions of problem analysis: problem finding and problem solving. Chapter 2, "The Problem of the Problem," emphasizes problem finding, and Chapter 3, "The Problem of the Solution," discusses problem-solving processes and strategies. The terms "problem of the problem" and the "problem of the solution" are from the writings of Professor Jacob Getzels. In Chapter 4, we discuss problem analysis relative to administration and provide some examples, problem scenarios, and exploratory ideas about relationships among problem analysis, leadership, decision making, and change. Chapter 5 contains some cases and vignettes, followed by a brief annotated bibliography, references, and appendices.

Although we include examples throughout the text, the early part of the book is more expository and didactic, whereas the later sections are more descriptive. In the text, a vignette is a fairly brief problem situation. A case study provides added detail and depth for analysis. We hope that readers will consider their own possible actions and reactions to these examples. The vignettes and case studies can be a foundation for group work and discussions using ideas expressed in the text.

PROBLEM ANALYSIS IN EDUCATION

Problem analysis is included as Domain 3 of the National Policy Board on Educational Administration's (NPBEA) book, *Developing Leaders for America's Schools* (Thomson, 1993). Problem analysis is an important domain of the principal's job, but until recently it has received little focused attention. Principals and other education administrators are different from business administrators or prison administrators in that their problem-analysis emphasis relates to education and not to economics or to corrections (although it is tempting to consider similarities). The generic definition of problem analysis that gives direction to this book is from the NPBEA (Thomson, 1993).

> **Problem Analysis:** *Identifying the important elements of a problem situation by analyzing relevant information; framing problems; identifying possible causes; seeking additional needed information; framing and reframing possible solutions; exhibiting conceptual flexibility; assisting others to form reasoned opinions about problems and issues.* (p. 3–3)

This definition suggests a pattern of problem analysis that can be conceptually linear to assist a person in the study of the problem-analysis process. In reality, however, the problem-analysis process is interactive and iterative, with several activities occurring simultaneously. By branching and looping through these steps, the problem analyzer moves toward a solution to the problem as framed.

Our task is to explain problem analysis and to support that explanation with research, theory, and exemplary practice ideas. Much in this book builds upon ideas and materials that have been researched by others, often for different purposes and in different contexts than education administration. Yet, principals can use many of these ideas to strengthen their own problem-analysis skills.

The focus of this book is, happily, problem analysis and not just problem solving. This is fortuitous for several reasons. First, people give serious attention mostly to problem solving because, in their minds, a leader's job is to rush in and solve problems, often with little regard to the consequences. The problem analysis format provides opportunities to consider "problem" in useful detail. Problem analysis and problem solving *are not* synonymous. Problem solving, like problem finding, is one part of problem analysis. Second, solving problems may create more problems or a different set of problems. The important distinction between problem analysis and problem solving is much at the heart of education's problems and criticisms today, as well as in the past. We try to explain this phenomenon.

Problem finding, the creative art and skill of ferreting out and shaping the real problem, must be expertly done if problem solving is to be productive and satisfying. This distinction in no way downplays the importance of problem solving, and particularly the skill with which expert problem solvers go about the task of solving problems. Expert problem solving is an important area of study and a major component of administrator preparation programs (e.g., Leithwood and Steinbach, 1995).

Problem solving is closely aligned with the scientific method, with a strong base in logical positivism and pragmatism. An obvious problem in a carefully logical approach to problem analysis is that problems in education often seem opinion or belief driven, and even chaotic or random. But before one gets to the actual problem-solving stage, there are complex precursor events.

Attitudes, beliefs, and values play major roles in problem determination and problem solving. For example, values and their attendant perceptions greatly influence what problems are identified, what problems a person chooses to act upon, and what data someone might accept as valid and as useful in solving the problem. Successful administrators, those people who engage in both management and leadership activities, analyze and understand problems clearly so that their problem-solving results will benefit the persons with whom and for whom they work. Principals are administrators and must do both leadership and management tasks well.

LEADERSHIP AND MANAGEMENT IN PROBLEM ANALYSIS

The distinction between management and leadership is not just semantic; it is operational and important. We reject the idea that leadership and management are part of the same continuum, with the usual connotation of good or important attached to leadership and management considered as less good or less important (Murphy, Hallinger, and Mitman, 1983; Achilles, 1992). The ideas of management and of leadership carry over conceptually into two major components of problem analysis: problem finding and problem solving. Consider Figure 1.1, which illustrates the view of management and leadership as opposites on the same continuum and places competing values on each concept (see also Murphy et al., 1983). This may not be a productive way to consider these two terms.

FIGURE 1.1. VIEW OF MANAGEMENT AND LEADERSHIP AS OPPOSITES ON THE SAME CONTINUUM

Leadership   Management
(Important)   (Less important)

Rather than the above linear situation, we believe that a principal performs both leadership (change-oriented and disruptive) and management (keep the organization operating smoothly) activities, and that management and leadership activities can each be evaluated as important or good, and as less important or less good. We believe that there are strong similarities between (a) administration and problem analysis, (b) management and problem solving, and (c) leadership and problem finding. The expert principal gets high marks (+) for management and for leadership. These conditions are shown in Figure 1.2, which illustrates management and leadership each on its own contiuum. Being on separate continuums allows relatively value-free estimates of each (see also Murphy et al., 1983).

FIGURE 1.2. MANAGEMENT AND LEADERSHIP EACH ON ITS OWN CONTINUUM

Positive (+)   **Negative (–)**

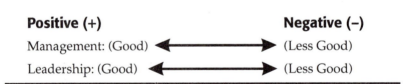

Management: (Good)   (Less Good)
Leadership: (Good)   (Less Good)

- A kindergarten child falls from a piece of equipment and breaks an arm. He does not tell the teacher or the assistant that he has hurt his arm. His mother threatens to initiate a lawsuit and to tell the media about the lack of supervision at the school. *How do both management and leadership play in this situation? How would you address this?*

The expert principal handles the routine, such as schedules, and also initiates changes to help the faculty reach the school's mission, perhaps by considering a new use of time to support instruction by moving to block scheduling from the typical 6- or 7-

period day. In the language of Figure 1.3, the highly successful administrator most often is rated as being in quadrant 1 (++). This person demonstrates superior leadership (problem finding) and management (problem solving) skills. Persons categorized in quadrant 2 have good management skills but fare less well in leadership ratings. Quadrant 3 includes good leaders who do not excel in management skills and detail work. Quadrant 4 presents its own sets of problems! As Figure 1.3 makes clear, the ideal state is quadrant 1.

FIGURE 1.3. MANAGEMENT AND LEADERSHIP SKILLS RATING

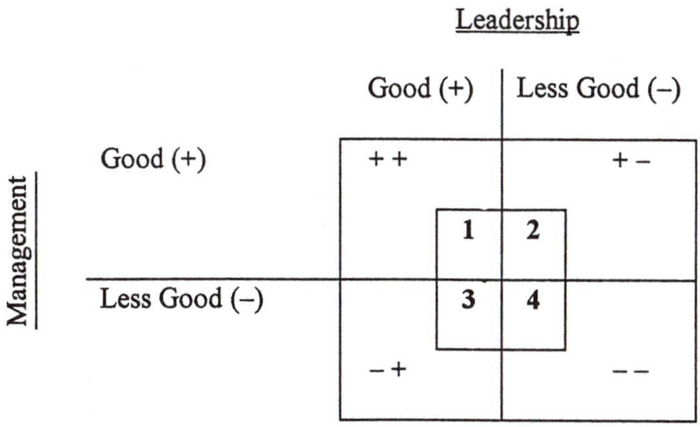

Leadership

		Good (+)	Less Good (−)
Management	Good (+)	+ +	+ −
		1	2
	Less Good (−)	3	4
		− +	− −

A good manager, while primarily concerned with expert problem-solving, may uncover glitches or problems in the ongoing processes of the school. A good leader, while primarily seeking improvement or new directions (problem finding), may establish important processes to keep the organization in what Lonsdale (1964) called "dynamic equilibrium."

Problem-solving steps, strategies, and processes can be taught. Most principals have had training in problem solving and in its logical implementation step, decision making. Where in their education process, however, and specifically in their education administrative preparation, did they learn problem-finding skills? Does preparation in problem finding fit comfortably into the formal curriculum of schooling at any level, or is it really the practical curriculum of living? Perhaps before seeking or finding a problem, a person should have a working definition

of "problem." This very point may be one cause of fuzzy problem solving.

PROBLEM: A WORKING DEFINITION

What is meant by the idea or concept "problem"? Rather
than relying on a narrow definition of a complex term, it seems
useful to consider similar terms that cluster around the idea as a
way to move toward a general understanding of a broad concept. Figure 1.4 provides one whimsical collection of terms and
ideas that may surround the concept of "problem." Figure 1.5 ar-
ranges some problem-analysis ideas into Getzels' conceptualization of the problem of the problem and the problem of the solution. The distinction between "problem of the problem" and
"problem of the solution" is important. Getzels said,

> Although there are numerous theoretical statements,
> a plethora of psychometric instruments, and quite lit-
> erally thousands of empirical studies of problem solv-
> ing, or what might be called the problem of the solu-
> tion, there is hardly any work of a similar nature on
> problem posing or what might be called the problem
> of the problem. (Getzels, n.d., pp. 4–5).

Clarity in understanding a person's use of the term "problem" is important, too. Unless people understand the problem
in similar ways, they will not communicate clearly or work har-
moniously on seeking a solution. Problem analysis includes
both problem finding and problem solving, and actively using
both concepts is one hallmark of a successful principal. Problem
analysis will lead to decisions, sharing of the problem and solution, initiation of some course of action, and eventual assessment of the outcomes of implementing a solution. The principal
will also help others understand the complexity of problem
analysis and assist them in forming reasoned opinions. The principal can grow personally in problem analysis through reflective thinking about the process, the solution, and the outcome.
These ideas are expressed in Figure 1.5.

Consider one source of misunderstanding in problem identification or problem framing. Person A describes a problem only
in terms of some discrepancy (e.g., 40% of the 9th graders at our
school are at or above the 50th percentile in reading on the XYZ
test). Person B believes that the discrepancy itself is not a problem but that it serves as an indicator that some problem exists.

FIGURE 1.4. SOME TERMS AND IDEAS RELATED TO THE CONCEPT "PROBLEM" (FROM A TO W)*

amazement	anxiety	astonishment	awe	bewilderment	bafflement
bugaboo	change	chaos	confusion	conundrum	difficulty
dilemma	discrepancy	dissonance	doubt	enigma	fear
frustration	gewgaw	gizmo	growth	hopelessness	issue
jejune	kettle of fish	lapse	maze	mystery	no-win case
obstacle	opportunity	perplexity	predicament	puzzlement	quandary
question	rebus	riddle	surprise	shock	topic
uncertainty	uneasiness	vexation	wonderment	worry	!*α Ω ?!
x?	y?	z?			

* We find that combining similar ideas to convey the concept of a term is more satisfactory than trying to express a single definition. Using the collection of ideas here and others that have eluded us, a person may construct a useful working definition of the idea of "problem." Perhaps some readers can get to the x-y-z of it.

FIGURE 1.5. ORGANIZING CONCEPTS AND IDEAS RELATED TO PROBLEM ANALYSIS (THOMSON, 1993, p. 33)

	Organizing Concept in Problem Analysis Definition	Ideas That Cluster Around The General Organizing Concept
Problem Of The	Problem Situation. Problem Finding.	Puzzlement, Dilemma, Discrepancy, Uncertainty, Problem Space. (See Ideas in Table 1.1).
Problem	Frame and Reframe the Problem.	Problem Finding, Problem Identification (ID), Problem Refining and Shaping, Information Search.*
Problem	Identify Possible Causes.*	Information Search. Check Reliability to Evaluate Data Being Received!
Of The	Seek New Information.*	Information Search. Consider "Frames of Reference" and Complementary Associations.
Solution	Frame and Reframe; New Solutions.	Reflecting, Analyzing, Developing. Scenarios. Asking "What if..."?
	Test Solutions. Evaluate.	Long-term Results; Short-term Outcomes. Feasibility/Reality Tests.
Problem Sharing	Exhibit Conceptual Flexibility.	Open Minded, Sensitive, Aware. Listening, Questioning. Staff Development.
Leadership In Decisions	Assist Others To Form Reasoned Opinions.	Consensus Skills. Seek Common Ground. Conflict Resolution. Adult Education Approaches.

* Information search is continuous: on causes, on possible solutions, on determining the efficacy of solutions. Information search is part of problem finding and of problem solving.

To person A, the problem is 10%; at least 50% of the ninth graders are not at or above the 50th percentile. To person B, whatever keeps the goal (50% at or above the 50th percentile) from being achieved is the problem. A semantic and philosophic battle over this point could needlessly hinder progress on problem analysis. To avoid this type of tension in problem analysis, we have accepted for this text the position articulated by person B:

> A problem situation exists when some discrepancy (uneasiness, dilemma, puzzlement, etc.) suggests or shows an unfamiliar situation or difference between a presumed better or desired state and the state that exists (status quo). To some, the problem situation is a dilemma that evokes problem analysis activities.

To be a problem of merit, the existing-state/desired-state discrepancy should be difficult to overcome and also be important enough to deserve the time, interest, and effort to resolve it (Smith, 1989a, p. 273; 1989b, p. 965). The presence of a problem situation or problem setting engages people and allows them to employ creative energy to identify a range of possible causes for the discrepancy or uncertainty, adding to the possibility that a correct, challenging, and creative solution will be achieved (that is, the more possible causes that are identified, the more potential there is for divergent and creative solutions).

THE DILEMMA AS A PROBLEM INDICATOR

Getzels (1979) described the dilemma and its relationship to problem finding and problem solving. McPherson, Crowson, and Pitner (1986) provided a clear discussion of the role of dilemma in problem finding. The main points in their discussion may help clarify the dilemma and problem-finding relationships:

> A dilemma thus is a perplexing, puzzling situation which attracts attention....Ominous clouds on the horizon interest the family driving toward the picnic ground...should the family drive back... home? Like most dilemmas, the storm is not the problem. *People cannot solve a dilemma, but must wrest from it a problem which is manageable, understandable, and potentially amenable to solution.*" (p. 274. Emphasis added.)

In schools, what issues are problems and what are dilemmas? Do principals really seek manageable "problems," or do they simply plug the dike of dilemmas?

The dilemma gets our attention. It can be represented by the actual, observable, and even measurable discrepancy between what we now have and what we desire, or by some event or fact that causes us uncertainty or unease about proceeding as we are now going. Something is, or soon could be, amiss, and the dilemma raises our consciousness about the uneasiness so that we become interested in taking some action. *The dilemma lets us know that a problem lurks nearby.* In the following vignette, consider the dilemma(s) and what might be the problem(s).

♦ A student has been diagnosed HIV-positive. The parents have a doctor's statement allowing the child to return to school. Other parents are aware of this situation and some are upset. They are concerned for the safety of their children and plan to protest this child's attendance. Some faculty members are also uneasy about the situation. *Dilemma? Problem? What action steps might you take?*

In the prior discussion of reading scores where only 40% of the students in school A read at or beyond the norm (50%), a negative 10% is a troublesome discrepancy, a measurable condition, and it poses a dilemma. This dilemma exists, and the professional educator must, to use the McPherson et al. (1986) term, "wrest from it a problem which is manageable, understandable, and potentially amenable to solution" (p. 274). In the problem finding and refining process in this case, a person with expert knowledge and experience in reading may have some advantage over a person not so equipped. Yet, the reading professional could have tunnel vision and try to define the problem in such a way that some pet theory or some program with possible personal gain would seem to be a preferred solution. (When a person has only a hammer, all problems look like nails.) Yankelovich (1991) warns us not to put too much faith in experts whose training, experience, and research may deter them from serious consideration of plausible alternatives (pp. 161–179).

THE PROBLEM SITUATION

The problem situation is the "playing field" for the problem finder where practice, experience, and often team work ("None of us is as smart as all of us") in using and refining the plays in the problem-identification playbook will lead to improved problem-framing skills. Figure 1.6 portrays the problem situation with some of its elements. The discrepancy between the is and ought dimensions generates disequilibrium that sets problem identification steps in motion. (Or the disequilibrium sets up a dilemma.) The steps of problem finding include

◆ recognizing the discrepancy

◆ studying and identifying possible causes of the discrepancy that signify a problem

◆ analyzing the possible causes of the problem (continue an information search into the evidence of the problem)

◆ beginning to connect potential solutions to various causes of the problem

Note the clear implication in Figure 1.6 that "problem" has no positive or negative baggage. A "problem" of improving an ex-

---

FIGURE 1.6. THE PROBLEM SITUATION IS THE ARENA FOR THE "PROBLEM OF THE PROBLEM"

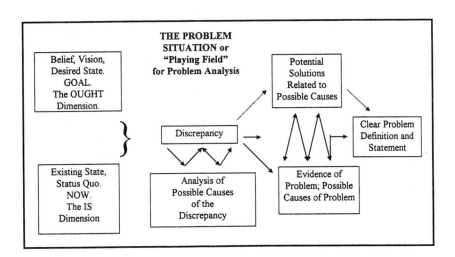

isting condition is as positive as rectifying some existing negative condition. Problem analysis is an opportunity to activate
one's creative and optimistic energy.

◆ People are encouraging you to add a "community
service" requirement. You study the students' current patterns of participation in school activities and
find (1) that most participation is by the same students, and (2) that these same students also generally have the better grades and deportment. *What is
the "playing field"? What seem to be the discrepancies?
Use Figure 1.6 to guide discussions of possible outcomes.
What is the problem?*

WHY TRY TO FIND PROBLEMS?

Everyone has problems. Different people consider problems
in different ways. For some, a problem is an opportunity, a challenge; for others, it is pain and hardship. In this text we emphasize problems that relate to management and leadership concerns encountered in the school milieu. As education expands
its role to include the "full-service school," for example, the principal will enter different political and social contexts and arenas.
Generalized education problem-analysis information will still
be useful, but that part of the information and skill base that is
context-driven will be elusive until the educator learns to navi-
gate in the new situations (Hoover and Achilles, 1996).

There is a body of literature and research on problem solving, but problem finding is a relatively new area of interest for
educators. In general terms, as administration includes both
leadership and administration, so problem analysis includes
both problem finding and refining and problem solving. Although each correspondence is not necessarily exact, some suggested relationships among problem solving, problem finding,
and other familiar terms are portrayed in Figure 1.7. Problem
finding is part of the principal's creative, change-directed, leadership activities. Although problem solving may contain creative contributions, it can be mostly routine, status quo, and technical in nature. These two dimensions (creative/routine)
converge with the implementation of a preferred solution to
yield positive, productive decisions that lead to school improvement. Without care in conceptualizing problems accurately, one
could spend considerable time solving and applying solutions

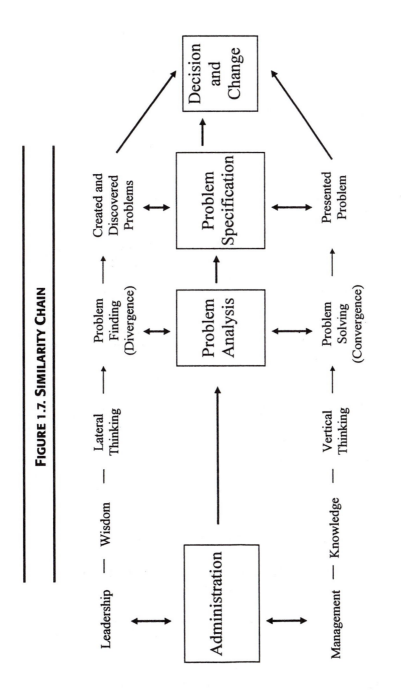

FIGURE 1.7. SIMILARITY CHAIN

to the wrong problem—or even to no problem at all—and this will be counter to advancing school improvement.

In a linear world, problem finding would always precede problem solving. The solving of one problem, however, usually generates new problems, and in this sense problem finding can be subsequent to problem solving. Since problem analysis can be learned, and once learned can be sharpened and refined through practice, much of the foundation for problem analysis and for its improvement comes from cognitive approaches to problems and to learning. In the challenging realm of problems, however, some things are beyond simply understanding and treating problems as facts. An aura surrounds the person who always seems to make the correct decision. Probably this embodies the dual notions of cognitive, the clear processing of data, and of affective, or having a "feeling for" the problem, or of having intuition about a course of action. Expert problem analyzers rely mostly on the cognitive elements, including experience, but will employ affective elements that are supported by intuition, tacit knowledge, or even serendipity.

Figure 1.7 provides a *similarity chain* approach to thinking about the concept of problem analysis. The similarity chain brings ideas together to focus on an issue. Rather than relying on one concept as a definition and pursuing the metaphor in depth, the similarity chain connects ideas to expand or broaden a person's range of thoughts. The pattern in Figure 1.7 adds concepts that may help define the complex relationships within problem analysis, and between problem analysis and other abstractions such as leadership, management, and change. Leadership, wisdom, problem finding, and discovered problems are closely related; management, knowledge, problem solving, and presented problems are closely related. A principal as administrator does both leadership and management activities in solving a problem and implementing a decision to change.

MINDFUL, METACOGNITIVE, AND PERHAPS EVEN INTUITIVE

Some principals have an eerie penchant for tiptoeing through a minefield of murky messes and for somehow always doing things right. Some sixth sense beyond the mindful, cognitive approach guides their every problem encounter. This might be coined as "tuned in," "lucky," or even "politically correct." Various people have called these metacognitive abilities ESP (extra-sensory perception), and have studied people who claimed to have them. For problem analysis, though, there may be less eso-teric explanations. Polanyi (1967) called one of these elements *tacit knowing*. For Polanyi, tacit knowing is the feeling for some-thing that you can't quite put into words in the usual sense. The following analogy concerns games where careful problem analy-sis aids the player to choose a successful line of play; that is, to move toward a winning choice.

The expert bridge player relies not only on the rules of the game, playing experience, and background information, but also on knowledge derived from analyzing bids that other peo-ple make in relation to the known cards in his or her hand and in the dummy. The accuracy of this analysis depends on an under-standing of bidding systems, of the cards in the deck, of the rules of the game, and springs from many years of thoughtful experi-ence in playing the game. In addition, the expert also under-stands nuances that aren't easily explained to the bridge new-comer; some nonverbal cue, a feeling, some nearly imperceptible movement, a fleeting expression. Whatever it is, the experienced player will factor that information into the cog-nitive structure developed from other elements of the same, such as the bidding, and so forth. But, and this is an important but, those nuances are not readily apparent and usable by some-one who has not first learned well the basics of the game. Apply the "rules of the game" in the following brief case study.

♦ **CASE STUDY: The Cheerleader Challenge**

You have been a principal at Ridgemont High School for 15 years. You are well-known and community people not only think well of you, but they also feel comfortable coming to you with problems that their children might be facing in your school. You have a young, energetic cheerleading coach, who has been at your school for 6 years and who has established a nationally competitive cheerleading program. Just this year, the varsity squad went to The National Competition and placed second runner-up. Now it is time for cheerleading tryouts again. The coach has ex-plained to those girls who wish to try out that there are rules inside the "Cheerleading Constitution" (that has been in place at your school for 15 years) that pertain to the conduct and reputation of those girls who will represent the school on the cheerleading squad. One rule states that, "No mothers or expectant mothers may be cheerleaders at Ridgemont High School due to the physical restraints and the time constraints involved." In the past, girls who could not meet this criterion were not allowed to try out for cheerleading.

Last night you received a call at home from a parent of a ninth grader who wishes to try out for cheerleading. Her daughter was told that she could not try out for cheerleading because she has a year-old baby at home. The mother complained to you that this policy was discriminatory, and that she would take care of her daughter's child while she participated in cheerleading for Ridgemont. She is threatening legal action if you do not look into this matter immediately. Further, this morning when you arrived at school, you received an essay written by the student in question stating that she was being discriminated against because she was a female and a mother. In the essay she questioned, "If football players can have babies and still play football, why can't I have a baby and cheer?" She explained that the doctor had cleared her physically and that she had appropriate and willing child care for her infant in the home. In short, she believes that she should be able to try out.

The cheerleading coach has confronted you with the "Cheerleading Constitution," pointing out that other girls have been denied opportunities based on this same rule; two that she can remember were African Americans, while this young lady happens to be Caucasian. The coach questions how she will be able to hold the squad accountable to other clauses in the Constitution, such as, "The reputation of a cheerleader should be above reproach" and "Cheerleaders should strive to be role-models in and out of the classroom," if mothers and pregnant girls are allowed on the squad. *What is the first thing that you need to do in this situation? How do you plan to solve this problem? What would you put into place to prevent this from happening in your school? Where could tacit knowledge or feeling play a part in this situation?*

So it is also with the decision-making principal who must understand clearly the problem in order to arrive at a preferred decision. This distinction is much like Polanyi's differentiation between focal and subsidiary cues; some things are just out of the cognitive range and become part of the equation peripherally as they enter through a "feeling for" or a sixth sense about the task. Tacit knowing incorporates the key concept that each of us knows things in our own area of expertise that are just a bit more than we can easily explain to an interested observer or novice. Some examples will make this point clearer.

Bookstores offer lots of good cookbooks. Many fine cooks write cookbooks. If all that a person had to do to be a great cook was to follow precisely the instructions in a cookbook, the world would overflow with great cooks. Yet, the few great cooks command handsome salaries and lavish praises. Why? The great cook knows more than just the recipe. The great cook knows the extra taste, touch, or feel that makes a good recipe into a great treat. Here's a down-home example.

Mother made great fruitcake. She made it in batches of 50 or more pounds, so she could give it to friends, and still have plenty for the entire year. People asked for the recipe, so she gave it to friends. But they still asked for her fruitcake. Why?

One year, in the hope of carrying on the tradition, I decided to help mother make a fruitcake. I followed the recipe exactly as it was written. After I blended all of the parts and the mix looked fine to me, I started to put the batter into cooking pans. Mother said, "Wait a minute, let me feel it." She put her hands into this 50-pound mass, kneaded it a little, and said, "It needs some flour." I pointed out that I had put in precisely the amount called for in the recipe. She insisted that it needed flour. I got a cup of flour. She said, "No, get me a teaspoon of flour." Frankly, I thought she had gone daft, and told her so. She asked me to put my hands in the mix and knead the batter. I did. She told me to concentrate on how it felt. I concentrated intensely on the "feel" of this huge mass. Then she added a teaspoon of flour, kneaded the batter for a while, added about another teaspoon of flour and mixed for a while. "Now feel the difference," she said. I did, and indeed there was a new consistency.

What let her know the difference and what did I lack? Some 40 years of experience in making fruitcake was a big part of it. She knew the general rules that she had written into a recipe; that was the equivalent of her policy book. The rules for this batch, however, were just a little different. Only the "feel," her tacit knowledge of fruitcake, identified the problem. Cognitive understanding of the rules plus a feeling for applying them made the difference between run-of-the-mill and expert fruitcake. Given the vagaries of administering today's schools, the fruitcake analogy may be innocently accurate!

♦ You receive a radio call from the school parking lot attendant that a student is leaning up against the building crying. The attendant states that the student refuses to come to the office. *What the principal does in response to this situation could indeed add the leavening to solving "the problem" successfully. The principal would have to have a feel for the "players" and the circumstances.*

These examples would surely appeal to Polanyi's sense of tacit knowledge. How does one define precisely that "it just felt right?" This feeling for a task or situation comes from a substantial knowledge of the essential basics plus years of experience in applying those essentials and recognizing that each context is its own problem. In the case of this fruitcake, perhaps some ingredients had slightly more moisture than usual; maybe the eggs were larger; perhaps I hadn't measured the flour exactly. "By the book" the fruitcake was correct; but "exactly" lacked something that was the difference between good and great fruitcake.

So it is with identification of problems and the selection of solutions. One can go only so far with cognitive understandings. The extra mile depends upon some understanding beyond the basics. Yet, without knowing the essential knowledge base, can a person even have opportunities to enjoy the tacit knowledge that comes with doing something well and of refining it as one does it? Our equation for problem analysis begins to unfold.

Expertness in Problem Analysis = *Cognitive Understanding*
 + *Tacit Knowledge*

Intuition is often called a "sixth sense." On occasion an intuitive response seems appropriate, but in relying on intuition one is confronted with what Wagner (1993, p. 94) called "the response biases of persons who respond to problems." One response bias is that administrators are prone to engage in wishful thinking, and they may urge intuition beyond its boundaries to support what they hope will happen. A second response bias is the "illusion of control," or the idea that the person working on the problem is in control both of the problem and of the outcome when, in reality, the person has little control. These two potential response biases can blunt the utility of intuition in problem analysis.

Tacit knowledge relates to information that one has but can't quite describe in regular language; *intuition is* a sixth sense that a person relies on without the cognitive and tacit knowledge that would be used in problem solving if it were available to the problem solver. *Serendipity* is when you get a correct answer but the facts and the processes are not really in tune with the answer. Experience is the expert problem analyzer's winning edge if used properly (Leithwood and Steinbach, 1995).

Consider the principal who lets students know that she or he is always just around the corner so the students should act accordingly. In effect, this principal is establishing an aura or myth. The secret is to make it work. ("The walls have ears.") The principal needs to be around the school reassuring students by being constantly visible.

♦ Third-grade students have a "gang" that is intimidating other students by using scare tactics. One student reports that in one instance the group demanded her lunch money. *What part could intuition, tacit knowledge or serendipity play in this situation? Why might experience be a first step in addressing this situation? What are other factors to be considered?*

ANSWERS MAY REVEAL THEIR OWN PROBLEMS

Does one really know the background of an answer someone else gives to a problem? Consider the primary school student who is asked, "How many hours are there in a day?" The student responds correctly. The teacher is pleased and praises the student for the correct answer, only to be taken aback by the child's further response: "I know there are 24 hours in a day. How many hours are there in a night?" So, what's the problem? Does the student not understand the term "day" or does the teacher not understand that the student doesn't understand? Either way, the correct answer was serendipitous. Sometimes questioning a correct answer will identify a problem. Problem analysis is difficult. The equation for problem analysis now is a bit more complete:

> Expertness in
> Problem Analysis   =   Cognitive Understanding +
>   Tacitness and Intuition +
>   A Dash of Serendipity +
>   Experience

THE CHALLENGE OF GOOD PROBLEM ANALYSIS: SCHOOL RESTRUCTURING AS AN EXAMPLE

Education seems to be interminably in the public spotlight; it is usually being criticized. Ineffective problem analysis could be part of education's negative media exposure. Examples from recent education history point out problems that really deserved careful analysis but received mindless solutions that may have been the "leap before you look syndrome."

The 1980s and 1990s have been a time of "restructuring" in education. Mitchell and Beach (1993) identified common themes in school restructuring activities, but they also challenged educators with the following question, "If restructuring is the answer, what is the problem?" (p. 266). Is restructuring such a ubiquitous answer that it solves all problems of education? One might say "yes," since so many schools and districts are doing it. Do all restructuring schools have the same problem and have all come up with the same solution? The improbability of this situation being true deserves careful scrutiny.

Is restructuring the answer for reduced student outcomes? For increased parental involvement? For improved student discipline? For improved school-community relations? Will restructuring make gangs go away? Will restructuring make teachers better? Will restructuring make leaders do what should be ethically done? These questions could go on. The point is, have the principals who are rushing to restructure seriously analyzed and defined the problems that they want restructuring to solve?

What restructuring plan solves which problem? Is all restructuring the same?

Perhaps the issue runs deeper. Has restructuring become a "bandwagon" effect? When business people realized that profitability was declining, they applied a series of steps to regain profitability, such as downsizing, merging, refocusing the organization, and using temporaries to save costs. The entire syndrome, called "restructuring," got national media attention and because it seemed to help some businesses make profits, some prophets suggested that restructuring would do the same thing for education. While some businesses restructure by downsizing, other businesses restructure by merging or getting larger depending on the problem. However, with little or no problem-analysis steps, some people argued that restructuring would save American education. Ogawa (1994) found that among change facilitators in the restructuring movement, educators were *not* major players. They were seen as little more than disseminators. Enter a new bandwagon, and everybody wants to be at the head of the parade!

Are there substantive data showing that restructuring has made a major difference in the primary goals and outcomes of schools as it may have helped businesses? The problems and goals are not the same for education and for business: "Business deals in dollars; education deals in sense!" (Achilles, 1990–1991, p. 36). If business and education have different goals, how do we know that the restructuring which helped business will help education? Who has analyzed the problems carefully enough?

If principals really believed that they were experts in education, would they have rushed to apply externally-proposed remedies to education before they understood the problem, the probable impact of various solutions, and whether a solution for business problems would apply directly to education's problems? Problem analysis takes on extreme importance in these situations. Try the following activity, doing it first alone and then with colleagues.

◆ Let's Share the Blame for Low Scores.

   The fourth-grade students were not doing well on their annual tests, and especially on the math. After several brainstorming sessions to settle on a way to correct the problem, school personnel contemplated a popular "effective schools-type solution" with a major focus on the students. Committees began to set this solution into motion. In the meantime, a deeper analysis of tests and test results revealed that the math deficiency was widespread and, specifically, that the primary deficit was in geometry concepts. The textbooks did include satisfactory information on the concepts that students were missing, so a curriculum alignment step did not seem needed. Next, almost as an afterthought, one administrator quizzed teachers about their knowledge of geometry and their approach to teaching geometric concepts. Many teachers admitted that they did not know geometric concepts well, so they either avoided teaching them or passed quickly over them. Student test scores rose markedly after the district sponsored a series of content-oriented workshops for teachers.

INCOMPLETE PROBLEM FINDING?

This result does not mean that some effective schools-type effort (e.g., focus on basic skills; hold high expectations for performance, etc.) might not also have led to some increased student test scores on math concepts, but it does show that how the problem is framed and analyzed will influence the solution that is considered and employed.

Consider this another way. Just because I have attended church does not make me an expert in religion; just because I was in the military does not make me an expert in military affairs; just because I have a bank account and pay taxes does not make me an expert in economic affairs. Just because people have been to school does not make them experts in today's education. As an educated person in a democracy, I am entitled to my opinions, but my "problems and solutions" for areas outside of education (my claimed expertise) should be taken only as suggestions and as ingredients for the crucible of public decision-making. In this model, the public (however defined) may identify concerns and problem situations. At this point, the professional or trained educator is called upon to analyze and to clarify the problem. *If educators do not clearly define education problems in education terms, education administrators probably have not served education well.* For too long, education administrators have accepted externally imposed solutions to problems that have been presupposed with little or no data. If educators expect to improve education, they must be serious about problem analysis.

CONCLUSION

Education researchers and exemplary practitioners have identified important things that should be part of good schooling, but if those in charge of schools do not implement what research has shown to work, education is destined to be little more than racing engines with slipping clutches. To test what results research and practice have shown and to evaluate their impact in schools, educators must implement the findings, establish rigorous evaluation designs, analyze the outcomes, and move on to new challenges and problems. Careful problem analysis is a major precursor to education improvement. Without a clear perspective of a problem and the ability to connect that problem to the purposes of education, those who would lead in education find themselves moving in circles, perhaps following the adage, "When in trouble or in doubt, run in circles, scream and shout."

The next two chapters, the "Problem of the Problem" and the "Problem of the Solution," examine two major elements of problem analysis: problem finding and problem solving. Careful attention to problem analysis and subsequent decisive action can straighten the path to improved schooling.

SOME EXERCISES TO INTEGRATE RAISED CONCEPTS

♦ What are the three to five most urgent problems you face as a member of an education organization? Write a short, one-sentence problem statement indicating the nature of each problem. Analyze each problem statement in terms of what you have learned in this chapter. Revise them, if necessary, until you believe that each statement truly represents the problem that exists. Choose one problem that you remember. Read Appendix A and, after the fact, using reflection, complete the Case Record worksheet using your problem as a focus.

♦ Ask a colleague who has also read this chapter to review your problem statements.

♦ Identify several problems that you have dealt with in the past. For each problem identified, and using Figures 1.5 (p. 8), 1.6 (p. 11), and 1.7 (p. 13) as guides, trace the problem from the time you first sensed it to the time you believe that you satisfactorily framed and addressed it, and then to the time that you made or implemented a decision to deal with it. Share this work with a colleague who has read this chapter, and discuss each other's problem-analysis efforts.

♦ Consider leaders or managers you have known in terms of their placement into one of the quadrants of Figure 1.3 (p. 5). Discuss the attributes that encouraged you to make the placement.

2

THE PROBLEM OF THE PROBLEM

In many fields, the solving of a problem gets rid of it or at least ameliorates it. If a doctor diagnoses appendicitis correctly, for example, and successfully removes the appendix, the patient is cured of the appendicitis. This is not so in education where solving one major education problem such as illiteracy or teaching people to read, write, and think may increase problems for educators. Thinking people will now seek more for their children. With their learned skills, educated people become educated critics of education, often creating problems at a higher and more complex level than if undereducated persons had raised the questions.

Administrator preparation programs usually contain courses in decision making, problem solving, change process, and leadership. Some skills and competencies from such courses are linked conceptually to problem analysis with its two main elements: problem finding and problem solving. The technical skills of problem solving form the basis of informed problem resolution, that is, of the problem of the solution. The first element in the problem-analysis equation, however, is a complex set of skills consisting of finding, defining, and refining the problem. This is problem identification or problem finding. Putting these two elements together (technical problem-solving skills and creative problem finding) provides the base for successful problem analysis and resolution that continues with decision-making, selecting and implementing a course of action, and evaluating the outcome of action.

All of this is problem analysis. Good problem analysis is an uncanny skill. The outcome of problem solving, one product of problem analysis, is usually a decision. The quality of a decision is results-oriented assessment of the administrator's ability in problem finding. Solving one good problem often creates other new problems and not solving the real problem *usually* creates more bad problems. Getzels' (1979, 1985) has shown that the "problem of the problem" leads inexorably to the "problem of the solution." Because the principal deals with people and with problems related to people, the principal has a role to play in educating others in the processes of problem analysis. Figure 2.1 portrays some components of problem analysis (level I) and subsequent actions that lead to action outcomes (level II).

In a 1985 article from the National Association of Secondary School Principals (NASSP) *Bulletin*, Getzels summarized some of his long-standing work on problems, and especially on problem finding as a creative and intellectual activity. Rather than try to convey these points secondhand, NASSP gave permission to reproduce a portion of that article on the next few pages. In reading and contemplating this material, translate the seminal ideas on problem finding to educational administration and specifically to administration in the organization where you work. Imagine how the key concepts could be applied in your setting. Thus, when Getzels says that a creative scientist or artist is identifying problems, imagine that the artist is a principal. The creative achievement or "product" for Getzels is a completed piece of art. For the principal, the "product" of problem finding is the result of problem solving—a decision or a plan of action. Getzels noted that problem finding was a new idea in education: "Despite our diligent search we were unable to locate any existing methods or in fact any prior studies of the subject."

Schools are remarkably common in most aspects: students, teachers, schedules, administration, all other personnel, curricula, support activities, and so on. What makes one school exciting and different from others? Might it be how problems are defined and solved? Might it be the uncommon arrangement and deployment of the common aspects? For one principal the problem is a drudge and a hassle; for another principal, the problem is an adventure and an opportunity.

The portion of the article is reprinted as it was published except for the present authors' musings and comments that are presented in brackets. The entire article is valuable, and you might wish to look it up. Problem finding is hard work and highly creative.

FIGURE 2.1. PROBLEM ANALYSIS AS PART OF LEADERSHIP FOR EDUCATION IMPROVEMENT

I.   Problem Analysis with its two main elements.

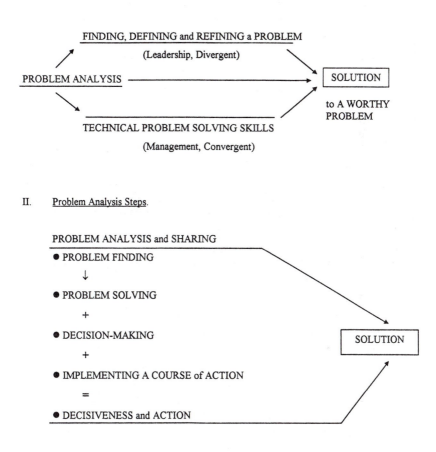

II.   Problem Analysis Steps.

GUIDING QUESTIONS AND INTEGRATING ACTIVITY

As you read this complex material, use the ideas in the following integrating exercise to build your understanding of the importance of problem finding. Share and compare your ideas with at least one other colleague.

- What, according to Getzels, are the characteristics of productive problem finding? What behaviors characterize the productive problem finder? How can a principal build these behaviors into his or her leadership style? How might a principal include problem finding in the required activities of staff development and community relations? What are the typical constraints that hinder a principal from creative, professional problem finding?

The following excerpt is reprinted from and courtesy of *NASSP BULLETIN*, Volume 69, Number 482, September 1985, pp. 55–61. At the time of publication of this work J.W. Getzels was R. Wendell Harrison Distinguished Professor Emeritus of Education and the Behavioral Sciences at the University of Chicago.

PROBLEM FINDING AND THE ENHANCEMENT OF CREATIVITY

J.W. Getzels

The author—who with his colleague, M. Csikszentmihalyi, recently completed a 20-year longitudinal study of artists from 1963, when they were students at the School of the Art Institute of Chicago, to 1981 when they were at mid-life—in this article focuses on one hitherto unavailable observation that seems to have important implications for the education of the gifted and in fact for the not-so-gifted as well.

Permit me to start by citing three comments: One is by a preeminent scientist, another by a distinguished psychologist who devoted a lifetime to the study of productive thinking, and a third by one of the twentieth century's foremost artists.

Albert Einstein: "The formulation of the problem is often more essential than its solution, which may be merely a matter of mathematical or experimental skill. To raise new questions, new possibilities, to regard old questions from a new angle requires creative imagination and marks real advance in science."[1]

Max Wertheimer: "The function of thinking is not just solving an actual problem but discovering, envisaging, going into deeper questions. Often in great discoveries the most important thing is that a certain question is found. *Envisaging, putting the productive question is often a more important, often a greater achievement than the solution of a set question.*"[2]

Henry Moore: "I sometimes begin drawing with no preconceived problem to solve, with only a desire to use pencil on paper and only make lines, tones, and styles with no conscious aim. But as my mind takes in what is to be produced, a point arrives where some idea becomes conscious and crystallizes, and then control and ordering begin to take place."[3]

The point that Einstein, Wertheimer, and Moore make is the critical role of finding and formulating problems in creative thought. [Emphasis added.]

[Authors' musings: Does a principal's urgency to act—perhaps on a nebulous or presented "problem"—contribute to the triteness and faddishness so often found in education? A presented "quick fix" is easier and flashier than creative problem finding.]

Prior to the emergence of the problem, there is no structure and no task; there is nothing to solve. After the problem is formu-

---

1. Albert Einstein and L. Infeld, *The Evolution of Physics* (New York: Simon and Schuster, 1938), p. 92.

2. M. Wertheimer, *Productive Thinking* (New York: Harper and Row, 1945), p. 123.

3. H. Moore, "Notes on Sculpture," in *The Creative Process*, edited by B. Ghiselin (New York: Mentor Books, 1955), p. 77.

lated, the graphic talent of the artist or the experimental skill of the scientist takes over; control and ordering begin.

> [Authors' musings: Problem solving is taught in preparation programs, but problem finding seldom is. Is a principal's need to control and to order things the compelling reason to rush to solve things before defining the problem?]

The crucial step is how a formless situation where there is no problem, or there is only an indeterminate dilemma where the problem is moot, is transformed into a situation where a creative problem for solution emerges. *For the quality of the problem that is formulated is the forerunner of the quality of the solution that will be attained.* [Emphasis added.]

Envisaging the fruitful problem—putting the right question—is surely not a lesser and is often a greater intellectual achievement than attaining the effective solution once the productive problem is posed. [Emphasis added.]

> [Authors' musings: Leaders seek problems, not just the chance to implement someone else's solutions to presented problems—to problems stated to accommodate the offered solution.]

This, in brief, is the anomaly to which I direct my argument: While instruction in schools is devoted almost exclusively to teaching how to solve what Wertheimer referred to as "set" questions or what we may call presented problems, the creative scientist or artist is deeply and often primarily concerned with finding and formulating questions or discovering problems worthy of solution, that is, with what we may refer to as the *problem of the problem* itself.

To get the process of creative performance and not merely catalog its biographical and psychometric correlates, we turned to observing how the creative artistic product, the drawing or the painting itself, was achieved. Our observations and conversations with the art students as they worked at their easels were at once fascinating and bewildering.

But we also observed what proved to be crucial: When advertising or industrial artists go into their studios in the morning, someone gives them a problem to work on, sometimes a problem as specific as producing an illustration for a cereal box. They could be more or less inventive in working on this, but only within the limits of the problem assigned. They worked on *presented* problems.

...the quality of the problem that is formulated is the forerunner of the quality of the solution that will be attained.

When fine artists go to their studios, they face a blank canvas, and no more. They have to find or create the problem to work on. They work on *discovered* problems.

As Einstein forewarned in science and Moore in art, finding and formulating the problem was an integral phase of the creative process. In order to understand or to describe the process, we had to observe not merely how an already identified problem is worked on toward a product or solution....We had to observe how the problem that will be worked on is itself, to use Wertheimer's term, found.

"FINDING" THE PROBLEM

To observe how a person goes about solving a problem, we may use one or more of the numerous instruments devised for this purpose:...But suppose we want to observe how a person "finds" a problem—how one discovers, invents, poses, or formulates a problem. What can be done?

Despite our diligent search we were unable to locate any existing methods or in fact any prior studies of the subject. We ourselves had to devise a way to observe how problems are found and formulated just as ways had been devised to observe how problems are solved.

What we did was to furnish a studio at the art school with two tables, a drawing board, paper, and a variety of dry media. On one table we placed a collection of 27 objects used at the school to construct still-life problems. We then asked 31 fine arts students, one at a time, to use one or more of the objects on the first table to create a still-life problem on the second table and to produce any drawing they wished of the still-life problem they had created.

We observed what they did in creating the still-life problem before they began the actual drawing and were able to differentiate how they went about formulating the problem on several dimensions—for example, the number of the objects examined, the amount of exploration of each object, the uniqueness of the objects used.

We assumed that to find or create an original problem rather than reproduce an already known or "canned" problem, one had to be open to a greater breadth of possibilities, to explore the objects in greater depth, and to consider the more uncommon objects.

> [Authors' musings: What determines a school's "personality?" Surely, the uncommon arrangement of "common objects" contributes to the uniqueness of each school and its leaders.]

We ourselves had to devise a way to observe how problems are found and formulated, just as ways had been devised to observe how problems are solved.

Our expectation was that the overt behaviors in this problem-finding situation would reflect meaningful underlying thought processes just as the overt behaviors in the familiar problem-solving situations are similarly taken to reflect underlying mental processes. If this expectation was unwarranted, or if our assumption about the role of problem finding in creative thought was invalid, the experimental results would "wash out" and there would be no relation between the quality of the problem finding and the quality of the ensuing product.

The procedure for examining the relation between the quality of the problem finding and the quality of the creative product—the completed drawing—was quite straightforward. We ranked the artists on the quality of their problem finding on the basis of the breadth, depth, and uniqueness of exploration before they began to draw. Needed next was a measure for judging the quality of the drawings....

COMMENTS AND OBSERVATIONS

The study I have reported here was illuminating beyond our expectations, as were a number of similar studies of problem finding in areas other than fine art. But...caveats must be mentioned:

First, problem finding and problem solving are not as discontinuous as my necessarily schematic account here may have implied; they meld into one another, and the problem may be altered in the process of its solution.

Second, to emphasize the importance of finding and formulating problems is not to diminish the importance of the skills needed for solving problems or the importance of the solution....

...finding and formulating problems is well worth educational attention not only as incidental to problem solving...but as an important focus of interest in its own right.

Nonetheless, a number of things may be said with some assurance: The discovery and formulation of problems can be studied empirically; individual differences occur in the finding and formulating of problems just as they do in the solving of problems that have already been formulated; and a positive relation exists between the quality of a problem that is found and the quality of the solution that is attained. The discovery and formulation of problems is a fertile field for further conceptual and empirical investigation. Some years ago, a number of the world's most distinguished scientists were brought together to consider the question: How can creativity be enhanced?

A variety of suggestions were made, and most agreed that creativity might be enhanced through apprenticeship to a successful scientist. But everyone without exception agreed that *the most important thing to be learned is how to ask the right question, pose the productive problem.*

...At the root of an answer is a question. At the core of an effective solution is a productive problem. This makes what I have referred to as the "problem of the problem" such an important subject for inquiry and instruction in our schools.

Portions from this paper are drawn from previously published work or from work in progress including: J.W. Getzels, "Creative Thinking, Problem Solving, and Instruction," in *Theories of Learning and Instruction,* edited by E.R. Hilgard. The 63rd Yearbook of the National Society for the Study of Education, Part I (Chicago: University of Chicago Press, 1964); "Problem Finding and the Inventiveness of Solutions," *Journal of Creative Behavior* (1975):12–18; "The Problem of the Problem," in *New Directions for Methodology of Social and Behavioral*

Science: Question Framing, edited by R. Hogarth (San Francisco: Jossey-Bass, 1982); J.W. Getzels and M. Csikszentmihalyi, *The Creative Vision: A Longitudinal Study of Problem Finding in Art* (New York: Wiley, 1976); M. Csikszentmihalyi and J.W. Getzels, "Creativity and Problem Finding in Art," in *The Foundations of Aesthetics, Art, and Art Education*, edited by F.H. Farley and R.W. Neperud (New York: Praeger).

THE PROBLEM/SOLUTION NEXUS

Viewed in a dual perspective, it is possible to have a correct or "good" problem or solution, and also a wrong or "bad" problem or solution. This idea is portrayed in Figure 2.2 with a touch of whimsy. The ultimate outcome in this conceptualization is found in quadrant 1—a correct or good solution for a correct

---

FIGURE 2.2 A PROBLEM/SOLUTION MATRIX
(P = PROBLEM; S = SOLUTION)

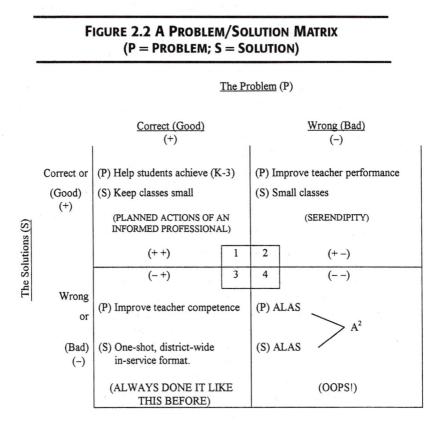

Figure 2.2. A problem/solution matrix. Quadrant 1 is ideal; quadrant 4 may be whimsical, but it is to be avoided. P = Problem. S = Solution.

and matching problem. Consider the widespread problem of increasing student achievement and improving student participation in school. Substantial research has shown the positive benefits for small classes (1:15) to obtain these desired outcomes (e.g., Finn and Achilles, 1990). Quadrant 1 in Figure 2.2 provides a good solution to solve a worthy problem. Quadrant 1 is ideal, while quadrant 4 may be whimsical.

It is possible to have a good solution that is serendipitously linked to a problem worthy of solution, but not the problem for which the solution was originally intended; the solution and problem were not truly aligned with each other so a "good" solution is connected to the wrong, but still worthy, problem. There is no research that shows that small classes harm students, so small classes could be considered a solution in search of a problem. A problem for principals is helping new teachers learn classroom management, their subjects, and teacher skills. New teachers, unfortunately, often get large and difficult classes in the worst schools as a rite of passage. Bright teachers soon leave and students get shortchanged. Suppose new teachers had "small" classes for their first year or two of teaching? See quadrant 2 in Figure 2.2. Here a good solution (small classes) found for one problem (student achievement) may be helpful in solving another problem.

Quadrant 3 includes much of education's operational mess. Problems that deserve serious attention are often crippled by poor solutions that may come from a lack of knowledge or inept problem analysis. Problems that deserve attention may not be clearly defined or they may become "presented" problems driven by ideology and not by professional knowledge. Consider the need for continuing professional development for educators but the use of one-shot, large-group meetings as the "cure." Consider the problem of dropout rates and policies to raise standards that lead to greater retention in grade with no provision for remediation. At issue here is Getzels' concern that poor problem-finding and refining skills and poor problem-solving are linked.

Quadrant 4 is a putative possibility, but probably not prevalent. (Principals might relegate to quadrant 4 those "crazy" issues brought forth to "save" education!) Poor solutions derive directly from inept problem identification. The "cure" for student achievement is longer school days (more of the same). Increase student attendance by making it mandatory that a student will fail a course if the student misses 10 or more days.

Of interest in the process of problem finding and its relationship to problem solving, as shown in Figure 2.2, is a research issue of "Type III errors" that has been transferred to other sectors, such as planning and decision making. Volkema (1986) summarized the idea:

> Differentiated from Type I and Type II errors (rejecting the null hypothesis when it is true and accepting the null hypothesis when it is false, respectively), the practice of entertaining the wrong hypothesis (i.e., solving the wrong conceptualization or a suboptimal conceptualization of the problem) [is] an Error of the Third Kind (Type III error). (p. 267)

This conceptualization includes not only the ideas of the right and the wrong problems, but also the idea that the correct problem could be less-than-astutely posed. Enter the role of problem finding, framing, reframing, and problem refinement. The result of problem identification is the emergence of a clear, correct problem statement that gives direction to problem solving. Lest anyone believe that problem finding and framing are value free and unimpassioned, Volkema (1986) pointed to the political dimensions of problem-solving techniques such as playing "the devil's advocate" or "assumptional analysis" that are designed to challenge the "premises, conditions, events or attributes that are taken as facts or 'givens' in existing conceptualizations, without necessarily offering a different statement of the problem" (p. 267). What problem is chosen, how that problem is stated, and even who states the problem all influence the later direction of problem solving and decision making. The scientific idea of problem finding and formulation may be a highly politicized activity aimed at some self-serving outcome or self-interest benefit, even to shifting the blame or saving face.

For example, if mathematics test scores are low in grade four, the grade-level chair may pose a problem that the scores are low because of low student motivation or inattention to homework. Here, the focus of solving the problem as identified will be on students—in effect, blaming the students for poor performance and absolving the teachers. The way that the problem is stated actually keeps the professionals from seeking alternative, and perhaps actual, problem causes. The dilemma or discrepancy (problem situation) is unacceptably low scores by grade-four students on math tests. There may be many possible solutions if the problem is stated well. A fairly neutral way to set the task and to avoid identifying a culprit at the start is to pose an objective or goal, and then to engage in careful analysis of barriers that might keep the goal from being achieved. Avoiding assessing blame in the problem statement is one way to encourage divergent thinking in considering the problem. A neutral goal might be, "To raise student math test scores in fourth grade by 10% over baseline-year scores by the next spring."

This neutral goal provides clarity and also a target. If problem solvers can get to the heart of the problem, they may move toward a successful solution. Problem solving requires data and action—not just any data and any action, but the *right* data and the *right* action for the *right problem*. The way the problem is defined shapes future actions.

INTEGRATING ACTIVITIES

Consider the following example and develop a clear problem statement that does not limit the range of problem-finding steps and does not limit the possibility of a correct solution. In the example, the way that the problem was framed after a discrepancy was found established the processes used to address it.

- ◆ The school system's organization was elementary (K–6), junior high (7–9), and high school (10–12). For several years, administrators noticed a large difference in discipline referrals to the office between sixth graders and seventh graders. Since the district had only one junior high school, the number of sixth graders in feeder schools was about the same as the number of seventh graders the next year. However, the discipline-referral rate for seventh graders was about 3.5 times that of sixth graders. Throughout the problem identification process, "discipline referrals" were the impetus for framing the problem, so the solution included a major emphasis on student indiscipline and on procedures for handling student behavior that went counter to the student code of conduct. Over several years of attention to student behavior and to discipline procedures in seventh grade, the discipline-referral rate difference between sixth and seventh grade was reduced from about 3.5 to about 2.0 times as many referrals in seventh grade as in sixth. Yet a large differential remained.

For a graduate class, one administrator surveyed teachers in the system to learn about the instructional methods that they used in their classrooms. The sixth-grade teachers used small groups, hands-on methods, and learning centers; all seventh-grade teachers employed large-group lecture and student note taking as the primary vehicle of instruction.

Might a change of instructional delivery—an element not even considered in the original discipline-rate issue—have an influence on the discipline-rate differences? Consider how different approaches to the problem might have reduced student indiscipline. Instead of posing the question, "What behavior management and student discipline strategies will reduce student referrals to the office?," a more general question such as, "What are the possible causes of the much greater discipline referral rate in grade seven than in grade six?" might have been considered. The emphasis in problem finding is divergent thinking rather than the convergent thinking used in problem solving. In the following case study, there are several interruptions for analysis and discussion to show some results of decisions made without clear problem analysis.

SETTING THE STAGE

Fran eagerly accepted the middle school principalship knowing that a key factor in being offered the job was a history of rapid, hard-driving, and forceful—if occasionally unpopular—decisions while serving as principal of the district's premier elementary school. If Fran had a key strength it was the propensity for action, the ability to cut through all of the nonsense, and to solve the problem. Darn right. Look at the record.

Two summers ago the school board was considering ways to save money and Fran had heard the politically upward-mobile board chair informally wonder why small children could not be in larger classes. After all, the chair mused, these little kids were easy to control and discipline problems should not get in the way of real instruction. So, before school started, Fran took action with firm decisions on two fronts that quickly won praise among persons who preferred the way things used to be. Fran cut three teachers by increasing the class sizes in grades K–2 and adding teacher assistants in the larger classes. This action saved money. Besides, the assistants lived in the school community and the teachers commuted. Hiring the assistants would help school-community relations. Two teachers were later rehired.

To address community pressure to increase standards and to get tough on low achievement, Fran quickly implemented the ideas offered by a small group of very active upper-income parents who often volunteered at school. Fran had asked teachers to "get tough" and to tighten up on grade retention in the early grades, particularly in grades 1 and 2. After all, as the parents had said, it made good sense that if a child had to be retained, the right time to do it was soon. The child should learn early in life the benefits of hard work.

Already Fran was thinking ahead about how to solve some problems that the local "Business Round Table," a group of prominent local business leaders who met monthly to suggest ways to make schools more "business like," claimed were rampant in the high school and had probably begun with those exploratory courses at the middle school. "What those unruly middle-school adolescents need," the business group opined, "is stricter discipline, drill in the basics, more expensive technology, and above all, a lot less exploratory stuff."

ANALYSIS TO THIS POINT

Analyze Fran's situation and actions to date. What trouble can Fran's propensity for fast and decisive action bring? Does Fran consider what research has shown about retention in grades, class size, middle-grade schooling? How have Fran's actions stacked up in an educational view? In a community view? Analyze the actions using the following problem-analysis equation:

Problem Analysis   =   Problem Finding
+

Problem Solving
↓

Action for Change
↓

New Problems

(↓ = *leading to*)

By stating the problem as they perceived it and also by urging a preferred solution, the business leaders had effectively usurped both Fran's professional problem-finding and problem-solving roles. That left only one element of problem analysis, one that Fran had a strong record in accomplishing—taking action. Fran had only to implement a decision to what Getzels (1979, 1985) has termed the "presented problem." The only part of the problem analysis equation that Fran had to solve was "action," and a history of fast and decisive action put Fran squarely in the driver's seat.

NOW, BACK TO THE CASE

Fran embodied action—a person who could make firm, fast decisions and then stand behind them. No wonder Fran's career seemed secure on a fast track to the central office. Those workshops Fran attended on decision making had some benefit, especially for people able to winnow the wheat from the chaff. Fran had always tuned out those egghead discussions about "problem analysis." That was all theory and "university professor fluff." What the community wanted, in fact what the community demanded, were common sense, decisive actions, and budget controls. Fran could deliver those.

CONTINUING ANALYSIS OF THE CASE

Consider the elements in the case when contemplating the following questions. Keep in mind that decisions based on evidence (data) are usually preferred to decisions based solely on opinion (everyone has opinions). Apply problem-analysis steps, especially problem-finding ideas, that have been introduced previously.

+ What problems was Fran "solving"?
+ Whose problems was Fran solving?
+ What are the bases for Fran's decisions—moral, political, symbolic, ethical, ...?
+ What new problems evolved from Fran's solutions, or what ones could evolve?
+ How would *you* begin to determine the problem or problems?
+ What other decisions might a group of professional educators offer for Fran's "problems" if the group engaged seriously in problem analysis?

Although exemplifying the person of action, Fran misses the mark as a professional and scholar-practitioner principal. Professionals have and use specialized knowledge to deal with problems of people, and the first rule of a professional is *primum non nocere*—above all, do no harm (to your client). Yet solid research has shown that some decisions that Fran so boldly made will not help—and probably will harm—the education of the pupils entrusted to Fran; those decisions broke the first basic rule of a helping profession. If Fran had engaged in problem analysis with a heavy dose of information search, some of the research uncovered would have provided directions for better decisions. For example, considerable research has shown the deleterious elements of grade retention (e.g., Holmes and Matthews, 1984; Shepard and Smith, 1986; Harvey, n.d.) and the positive benefits of reduced class sizes in elementary grades (e.g., Glass et al., 1982; Finn and Achilles, 1990; Mosteller, 1995). Solid problem analysis could have shown alternative paths to gain consensus and to demonstrate Fran's leadership in professional matters.

Questions: Is Fran male or female? Does it make a difference? If so, why?

CONSIDERING GETZELS' IDEAS OF PROBLEM

From the numerous problem types that he had studied, Getzels (1979) proposed three broad problem categories: the *presented problem*, the *discovered problem*, and the *created problem*. Figure 2.3, which is excerpted from Getzels (1979), summarizes these three problem categories and shows the differences in how the problem is formulated (and by whom), the differences in the certainty of the method of solution, and the differences in the complexity of the projected solution. In the presented problem there is little problem-finding challenge for the person who is expected to "solve" the problem. Recall the case of Fran, the decisive principal with the propensity for action, as you read about the presented problem. The discovered problem condition is of key interest to the professional educator.

PROCEEDING ALONG THE PROBLEM-FINDING PATH

Given data, a machine can be programmed in the technical processes of solving a problem. In fact, given good or correct data the machine might even arrive at a good decision. This is not enough. Thoughtful solutions to problems require data, information, knowledge, and even wisdom. Knowledge and wisdom are more than technical competence and will increase the possibilities of arriving at good solutions. But a key question remains: good solutions to what?

Problem solving is a rewarding technical skill, and part of successful administration is the principal's use of proven technical skills. Although problem solving can be interesting, the real excitement and challenge in administration are determining or defining the problem and selecting the correct problem for the administrator and the rest of the group to work on and solve. Recall the long Getzels' quote presented a few pages ago: problem finding is a challenging, creative act. Part of administration is creative leadership.

FIGURE 2.3. PROBLEM CATEGORIES

- *Presented Problem Situation.* The problem is given to the problem-solver. It has a known formulation, known method of solution, and known answer. (This situation prevails in schools. Given that the side of a square is 4 feet, what is the area?) This is not really a problem in the sense of professional problem analysis. It only requires implementing someone else's solutions.

- *Discovered Problem Situation.* A problem exists and it is formulated by the potential problem solver, not by someone else. It may NOT have a known formulation, known method of solution, or a known solution. It meets the conditions discussed in this chapter in that it is amenable to refinement and offers a problem-finding challenge. Why do children, at about grade three or four, begin to dislike school when almost all children are initially eager to attend school? Does this American phenomenon exist in other cultures?

SYMPTOMS VERSUS PROBLEMS

You have heard someone say, "We're not treating the problem; we're only addressing the symptoms." Medical science still can't cure some diseases, but doctors provide relief by treating symptoms. In many instances, educators may be treating more symptoms than problems. Sometimes treating only symptoms will increase the problems.

One example of treating symptoms and not problems derives from education reform movements. Some people, usually noneducators, would have educators believe that failures in education cause U.S. economic setbacks. Some critics suggest remedies such as restructuring, raising standards for teachers and pupils, adding more subjects, adding more time to the school day, and adding days to the school year. Yet, each solution to an ill-defined problem brings new attendant problems. An increase in standards with no accompanying emphasis on remediation, which may cost money, will lead to more drop outs and more retention in grade. Both conditions bring their own problems. High dropout rates are linked to teen pregnancy, crime rates, violence, drug use, and high youth unemployment. The "gloom and doom" scenario marches on. Teen pregnancy, usually accompanied by inadequate pre- and postpartum care often results in low birth-weight babies, and low birth weight is a major indicator of at-risk children requiring high-cost special education services in schools. Who will pay? The price for treating symptoms rather than problems may be higher than the price of serious problem analysis.

"SCHOOLISH"-TYPE AND WORK-TYPE PROBLEMS

Most people in problem-solving situations or people who hold positions in which problem solving is part of the job have experienced academic problems during their formal schooling. Academic problems resemble Getzels' (1979, 1985) presented problems, as they have known answers, accepted methods of solutions, and are given to the student by a teacher. Academic problems are pretty cut-and-dried, but real-life problems are not usually routine. Wagner's (1993, p. 96) differences between academic and practical problems are paraphrased in Figure 2.4. Note the similarities between Wagner's ideas (Figure 2.4) and Getzel's ideas (Figure 2.3).

FIGURE 2.4. ELEMENTS OF WAGNER'S DISTINCTIONS BETWEEN ACADEMIC AND PRACTICAL PROBLEMS

Academic Problems	Practical Problems
♦ Well-defined and stated by someone else	♦ Identified by the person involved
♦ Defined and presented by someone other than the expected problem "solver"	♦ Defined by the person who encounters it
♦ Known solution and method of solution	♦ Solution and method of solution are determined by the problem
♦ All needed information is usually provided or evident	♦ Information search and analysis are required

---

According to Leithwood (1995), a problem is *routine* when (1) the present state is known, (2) the desired state is known, and (3) the procedures to get from present to desired are known (pp. 118–119). If one or more of the three conditions is not known (or is not known well) the problem becomes less structured. Peterson (1986) described two general classes of problems that encompass most concepts described by Getzels, Wagner, and Leithwood. The similar positions of the four authors help validate the concept of the two problem classifications. Figure 2.5 shows the conceptual differences between "problems" that require little problem finding, and true problem finding.

FIGURE 2.5. SUMMARY OF FOUR POSITIONS SHOWING THE SIMILARITIES OF THE PROBLEM TYPES DESCRIBED

Author	Problem Dichotomy	
	A	*B*
Getzels (1979)	Presented Problem	Discovered Problem
Peterson (1986)	Routine, Simple, Structured, Old	Nonroutine, Complex, Unstructured, New
Wagner (1993)	Academic Problem	Practical Problem
Leithwood (1995)	Routine, Well-structured Problem	Nonroutine, Ill-structured Problem

A key point to be derived from this analysis of similarities in conceptualizations of problem types is the leadership role required in clear problem formulation. This role is especially crucial in the real-life problems prevalent in column B of Figure 2.5. Working with people and the concerns of people is not the serene situation implied by conditions in Figure 2.5, column A.

FRAME, REFRAME, AND REFINE THE ISSUES

Problems take many shapes. Bolman and Deal (1993) posed four main "frames" for guiding the way that people look at problem situations, especially in organizations where people interact in structured ways. The same problem can take different shapes if it is framed in different ways or viewed through different lenses. When confronted by a dilemma that eludes easy problem definition, it may be useful to view the situation through different frames and compare the problems that emerge from each frame.

If you view things in a political frame, you will consider the political ramifications in solving this problem in a particular way. When framing the situation through a moral lens, you may ask, "What is the correct or right way to solve this problem in these circumstances?" Emphasizing the value structure will guide the solution, since ethical and moral issues are important; however, the solution may be assailed by competing value structures. If the primary value is "safety first," then a decision to construct a school building on a particular site would depend heavily upon the safety factors (values) involved. Yet, if important political interests own a key piece of property that they propose to sell to the school at a big profit, value or profit versus values or some moral belief that guides action will become important. If an overriding value involves child welfare, then knowing how to include health in the curriculum and to make health services available within the school building would be particularly important.

Using different frames helps a person analyze the problem situation to improve the possibility of clearly defining the problem and of arriving at a good solution. A principal could consider a problem situation in terms of one particular "frame," and then project various decisions and their potential results using that one frame as a base. If there is time, analyzing the problem situation through two or more frames and trying to find a common ground for the best solution will yield more rewarding solutions than by using only one frame of reference. The time and urgency considerations surrounding the problem will influence this process. Framing or reframing the problem, considering the philosophical or behavioral elements, projecting the impact of potential solutions, and reflecting on outcomes are important steps in acquiring expertise in problem analysis. Figure 2.6 is a suggested matrix usable to focus the problem analysis process. It shows how a useful matrix can be developed to guide a

FIGURE 2.6. "FRAME(S)" AS A VARIABLE IN A MATRIX TO GUIDE PROBLEM ANALYSIS

Other Factors	Political	Human Resources*	Symbolic*	Structural*	Legal	Moral	Etc.
Attitudes							
Beliefs							
Values							
Etc.							

* From Bolman and Deal (1984).

principal in comparing problem-analysis results from various frames. Use Figure 2.6 as a worksheet for analyzing the vignette, "Let's Share the Blame for Low Scores" (Chapter 1). Refer to Bolman and Deal (1984) if you need a discussion of the frames marked with an asterisk (*) in Figure 2.6. For each frame represented in Figure 2.6, provide examples of the attitudes, beliefs and values one expects to find among the decision-makers.

The discussion of frames may sound linear, but in fact several frames may come into play at the same time. As Getzels and Guba (1957) stated, some things are conceptually independent but phenomenally interactive. That is, they may be considered one at a time in a linear fashion; in fact, they are complex, interdependent, time sensitive, and interactive. A school problem contemplated through the political frame may also be equally based upon a value judgment relative to student safety.

THE ROLE OF COMMUNICATION IN PROBLEM FINDING

To analyze problems accurately and to solve them well, the problem solver must understand the problems clearly. Often the information related to a problem is oral or written communication. In face-to-face communication, nuances of the degree, bothersomeness, intensity, truthfulness, and so on, of the problem will be conveyed by nonverbal communication cues. The problem analyzer needs to attend carefully to meanings conveyed by nonverbal cues. This can sometimes be difficult because of communication differences between diverse groups. Communication cues such as posture, eye contact, spacing and distance, and so on, convey the affect (e.g., deference, hostility,) surrounding interpersonal investments in the problem and its clear definition. This topic warrants a volume of its own, and the reader should reference Muse, I. (1996), *Oral and Nonverbal Expression* (Larchmont, NY: Eye on Education), for a fuller treatment of some of these key ideas. The words convey only a portion of the total message. The affect of the situation may be transmitted by vocal cues such as tone, speed of delivery, pitch, and volume, and by personal cues, sometimes culturally and/or gender related, such as use of time, space, light, personal grooming, facial expressions, gestures, and eye contact. It is possible to hear—even to understand—the words in a message yet still not comprehend the full meaning of the message. Problems can be missed, misconstrued, or even blown out of proportion by poor communication. Written communications are more precise than are conversations. They are lasting and can be analyzed and studied repeatedly. People seem to take written communications more seriously than they take the spoken word. Written communications allow the problem finder time to consider the problem from several perspectives.

Inattention to nonverbal communication is a major obstruction to problem analysis and so are poor listening skills. Considerable "intake" for problem analysis will come aurally, but few people have had extensive training in listening. People who do not listen carefully (active listening) and translate accurately into action what they hear may commit errors in problem analysis. The process of listening and interpreting what a person hears is a key link in the chain connecting problem finding (identification) and problem solving.

The principal's role in active listening is important enough to problem analysis to warrant mention. Most people spend more than half of their communication time as listeners but because principals are expected to "be in charge" or to "do something," many focus more on talking, giving, and transmitting information. Yet, good problem identification requires much intake and processing of information. A principal's take-charge attitude—the rush to a solution—may dull the contributions of active listening and of reflection. Figure 2.7 summarizes some hints for improving listening skills. These can be honed by conscious practice, reflection on performance, and corrective actions. Listening well will benefit the listener, but it is most effective when it supports and enlarges the speaker. A good listener builds the esteem and self-confidence of the speaker while obtaining the information needed to improve problem analysis. The skill of listening and really hearing is not easy; it requires conscious attention and practice.

PROBLEM FINDING IS CREATIVE: HAVE SOME FUN, TOO!

This chapter began with Getzels' discussion of problem finding (the discovered problem). Other writers have had similar ideas, although their exact terms may be different. In Figure 2.8, the concepts of three writers are compared to show a "similarity chain." After the similarity, a syllogism presents the ideas as

FIGURE 2.7. STEPS TO IMPROVE LISTENING SKILLS AND TO SHARPEN YOUR INTAKE SYSTEM FOR PROBLEM ANALYSIS

Activity	Sample Do's	Sample Don'ts
PRACTICE *ACTIVE* LISTENING	*DO*: Paraphrase and verify; seek and provide feedback; ask questions to clarify; listen with feeling. Use "I" messages. Take time to hear.	*DON'T*: Interrupt or think about something else.
LISTEN WITH AWARENESS	*DO*: Remember the difference in speaking and listening speeds (about 1:3 or 1:4) and avoid tuning in/out. Take only a few notes of key points.	*DON'T*: Daydream, do other things (e.g., read a note) simultaneously, try to "mindread" or second guess, or prepare your response.
LISTEN WITH EMPATHY	*DO*: Try to experience the speaker's message and walk in the speaker's shoes. Support, not challenge, the speaker.	*DON'T*: Patronize the speaker, or put down the idea, or refuse to acknowledge an idea.
LISTEN WITH INTEREST	*DO*: Watch and listen for nonverbal nuances of affect.	*DON'T*: Lump or categorize issues. Ask emotional questions.
LISTEN WITH OPENNESS & ACCEPTANCE	*DO*: Judge the message through the speaker's frame of reference; consider the plausibility of another idea.	*DON'T*: Prejudge, filter ideas through your perceptual screen; judge the message by the speaker's delivery or appearance.

FIGURE 2.8. SOME SIMILARITIES ABOUT PROBLEMS AND THINKING (SIMILARITY CHAIN) (ADAPTED FROM ACHILLES AND NORRIS, 1987–1988, P. 106)

Barnard (1936)	De Bono (1971)	Getzels (1979)
Logical Thinking	*Lateral Thinking*	*Discovered Problem*
May know the solution, but seek the truth. Ask WHY?	Searching for questions. Ask WHY? Originate an idea	Problem seeker. Find a new problem or question. Ask WHY?
Nonlogical Thinking	*Vertical Thinking*	*Presented Problem*
Seek solution. Ask HOW? Persuade. Select a course of action.	Searching for answers. Ask HOW? Develop an idea.	Problem solver. Ask HOW? Use known method to get known answer.

The above dualisms provide the base for a syllogism:

I.   A. Leadership is proactive and seeks change.
    B. Problem Finding is proactive and asks "Why?"
    Therefore, Leadership is Problem Finding.

II. A. Management seeks a calm status quo and asks "How" to do things better.
    B. Problem Solving seeks ways to make present things better.
    Therefore, Management is Problem Solving.

III. A. Most education administration preparation Programs emphasize Problem Solving.
    B. Few education administration preparation Programs emphasize Problem Finding.
    Therefore, ...?

---

they relate to management and to leadership, the two main elements of administration. The principal is an administrator, so the principal must be good both at management and at leadership, and at both problem finding and problem solving, which combined constitute problem analysis.

In the article reprinted earlier in this chapter, Getzels (1985) noted the *creative* act of problem finding. Along with creativity goes the idea of having fun with problem finding. Practice the creativity and fun of problem finding by reviewing problems and the chosen solutions used in prior times. What alternative solutions now seem realistic? Then, reconceptualize the problems; think about them differently. This activity may help you see that problem finding can be challenging, creative, and fun.

Look around at tensions and fads in education today. Ask, "What if...?" The results may interest you. In his 1978 Walter D. Cocking Lecture to the National Conference (now Council) of Professors of Educational Administration (NCPEA), William Caudill challenged the audience with a list of irreverent, outrageous "what ifs" (Figure 2.9). From 1978 to now, many of these "what ifs" have spawned problems, "solutions," and more problems. For example, in thinking about a "Return to Basics" (item 6) consider the far-right, family-rights groups that are against a humanistic curriculum, definition of "the basics," and so on. If music and art were around before "readin', ritin', and rithmetic," are they the basics? Review Figure 2.9 with the wisdom of 20–20 hindsight and share a chuckle or shed a tear! Were these "what ifs" of 1978 problems or solutions then? Now?

FIGURE 2.9. "WHAT IFS" TO CHALLENGE EDUCATION ADMINISTRATION

---

1   WHAT IF we didn't have compulsory education?

2   WHAT IF taxpayers refuse to pay high and higher taxes to support public education, provoking more strikes and shutdowns?

3   WHAT IF the elitists are right when they contend that half of high school graduates shouldn't go to college?

4   WHAT IF instead of good management, educational administration implies innovative, spiritual leadership?

5   WHAT IF consumerism relating to education becomes stronger and patrons demand teaching performance in academic-related subjects such as grammar, creative writing, history, and mathematics as they now do in sports and band?

6   WHAT IF people demand a return to basics?

7   WHAT IF adult learners demand adult-centered schools or a mixture of adult-centered and child-centered schools?

8   WHAT IF the two-way cable TV concept is successful?

9   WHAT IF energy shortages become as critical as some experts believe?

10   WHAT IF administrators are authorized to clamp down on absenteeism, lack of discipline, vandalism, tardiness, and drug use?

11   WHAT IF government decides to throw more social service responsibilities on schools?

12   WHAT IF good people continue to abandon education becasue of low pay, physical abuse by older students, parental pressure, and disgruntled taxpayers?

13   WHAT IF patrons conclude that educational standards have slipped at all levels, from kindergarten to college, and that there must be competency tests, particularly at the secondary school level, toward formal assessment—not just a diploma based on course taking?

14   WHAT IF it's true that the quality of public education is on the decline?

15   WHAT IF overreaction occurs, negating the beneficial innovations of the last four decades, such as open classrooms, team teaching, flexible scheduling, use of electronic equipment, individualized curriculum, and integrated subject matter?

16   WHAT IF the critics are right who insist schools of education are doing a lousy job of preparing young people for the profession and an even worse job in further training of those who hold tenured positions?

17   WHAT IF there is a down trend in the marketplace for educational administrators?

(Source: Caudill, W.D. (1978). "Notebook for the 1978 Walter D. Cocking Lecture," in Bredeson, P., Achilles, C. And Strope, J. (eds.) (1988). Distinguished Lectures Presented to the National Council of Professors of Education Administration (NCPEA). Memphis, TN: NCPEA at University of Tennessee, p. 54.)

As part of the creative form of problem finding, consider the problem-finding steps in Figure 2.10 that could be the basis for a brainstorming session among education personnel. Some examples in Figure 2.10 purposely are not from education. Choose a prevalent issue from education and move it through the six steps in Figure 2.10.

FIGURE 2.10. SIX PROBLEM-FINDING STEPS TO IMPROVE PROBLEM-ANALYSIS EFFORTS

---

1   DREAM DREAMS—DREAM THE IDEAL AND ASK "WHY NOT?"
    Why not remove retention in grade as an option?

2   CHALLENGE COMMON PHENOMENA: WHAT IF...
    Screws were left-handed?
    Congress had to follow its own laws?
    Time in schools was not divided into small blocks?
    Education "standards" reduce teaching to accountability of testable skills?

3   ASK IRREVERENT QUESTIONS
    Why do we still have the penny (1 cent)?
    Why aren't postage rates easy to understand?
    Why aren't all schools open on a 12-month schedule?
    Why are "common" practices not common?

4   DO A LITERATURE SEARCH TO LEARN ABOUT A TOPIC
    Note gaps and find "glitches" in the available works.
    Do a discrepancy analysis.

5   FIND PATHWAYS—WRITE SCENARIOS, USE FUTURISTIC APPROACHES, AND REFLECT
    Frame possible actions in various ways.

6   DEVELOP "SIMILARITY CHAINS" TO HELP YOU CONSOLIDATE IDEAS ON ISSUES AND TO LOCATE PROBLEMS

Successful leaders actively seek problems to solve before the problems become visible to other people. Rather than, "If it ain't broke, don't fix it," they believe that, "If it ain't broke, break it, and study it." Reactive people may solve problems, but they often find themselves solving someone else's problems or even just implementing someone else's solution to that problem, thereby creating problems that did not exist before.

START THE PROBLEM-FINDING PROCESS: INTEGRATING ACTIVITIES

Some people don't recognize a problem-finding opportunity when they see it. Problem finding requires a forced change in thinking. Choose a colleague and try the activities below. Share and discuss your ideas. See Figures 2.9 (p. 52) and 2.10 for more models. For each activity, and also for each perplexing education event you encounter, apply these divergent steps.

♦ Ask WHY?, WHY NOT?, WHAT IF? for each item.

♦ Don't just look around; look up and around and wonder.

♦ Ask questions. Ask more questions. Question your answers.

♦ Turn things upside down, inside out, backwards in your mind.

♦ Think in metaphors and similes. Expand those. How does good schooling use the principles found in well-run businesses—only more so? How is education like part of Robert Frost's epitaph, a "lover's quarrel with the world"?

♦ Seek similarities and/or differences that "correlate" well. If there is high pupil absenteeism, how is teacher attendance?

♦ Study data, such as demographics, and ask, "What do these data mean for this school and the students in it?" Using demographics, establish problem situations for educators. The following scenarios could be sources of problems from demographic trends.

ACTIVITIES: FIND PROBLEMS BY USING STEPS LISTED ABOVE

♦ In California, the present minority, people of color, will be the majority by the year 2005. How do we know? Because today most California elementary school pupils are people of color. Educators can look at that group and begin to understand the change forces. In 1980, the U.S. Census Bureau predicted the U.S. population in 1985 within one-fourth of one percent! (Hodgkinson, 1986, p. 273)

Visualize the senior class of 2010 or so. How old are its members now? With no massive immigration, those youngsters are the only candidates for that senior class. What percent will become seniors? What percent will graduate? What will happen to the others? Of the 3.6 million or so 5-year-olds in 1987, the following facts were true (Hodgkinson, 1991, 1992). As demographers point out, "Demographics is destiny."

- About one-fourth of the group is living below the "poverty line."
- Far fewer are white, suburban, and middle class than in 1970. (The greatest birthrate decline is for the group that has usually made up a college freshman class.)
- About one-third of the group is nonwhite.
- Almost half will be raised by a single parent before they are 18.

♦ Consider this situation, again adapted from Hodgkinson's data. Teen mothers tend to have low birth-weight babies, and low birth-weight is an excellent predictor of major learning difficulty when a child enters school. This means that "about 700,000 of the annual cohort of 3.3 million babies (over 21%) are almost assured of being either educationally retarded or difficult to teach and in need of special education services." (Hodgkinson, 1985, p. 5) This fact begs for clear problem resolution.

What other problems might scenarios built upon demographic data reveal? Where in a principal's busy life is there time to think about finding problems? Leadership means working with Getzels' (1985) discovered problem—that is, attending carefully to problem finding. The quality of the problem will determine the quality of the solution. *The implications of this axiom should turn action-oriented problem-solving principals into problem finders.*

3

THE PROBLEM OF THE SOLUTION

Thinking and analysis entail specific mental skills that can be taught and learned. Working toward the problem of the solution involves an important subset of thinking skills. Moreover, professional problem analysis requires a special pattern or configuration of thinking and analysis. For principals, problem analysis is a daily issue. Lend an ear to Professor Kingsfield's classic speech at the beginning of the film, "Paper Chase," which ends with the statement that when you finally come of age in this great profession, "You'll be thinking like lawyers." Do lawyers actually use a process or procedure for thinking that differs from ordinary people's processes? Do doctors, engineers, architects, and other professionals think in special ways? These professionals think in problem-analysis/problem-solving modes that differ dramatically from how nonprofessional people think about problems, and it takes extensive, arduous training and practice to learn a professional mode of problem analysis (Reynolds and Silver, 1987).

In the ordinary course of events, to the extent that people think consciously about something (as opposed to thinking intuitively, behaving habitually, or reacting reflexively), their mental processes are influenced by an immense range of experiential and situational factors. To even imagine thinking in a new way, people must recognize at least some factors that shape how they think about problems of practice.

One important set of factors includes the norms and values prevailing in the social setting. For example, schools are typically viewed as bureaucracies having legitimate hierarchies of authority, rules and regulations, subordinates, leaders, and so forth. This view of schools carries with it a whole cartload of values and assumptions that shape and constrain the thinking about schools and school-related issues. Administrators as bureaucrats may value action over reflection, decisiveness over flexibility, loyalty and obedience over creativity, predictability over deviance.

But the bureaucratic model is not the only one available to describe schools. A professional model might be more fitting. In some other professions, values include recognizing problems and defining them clearly, experimenting with promising new procedures, testing assumptions against facts, enjoying the intellectual challenge of finding creative solutions to nagging problems, and recording actions in meticulous detail. These values provide a fertile ground where problem-solving skills can flourish and multiply.

Another factor that shapes and constrains problem analysis is the language used in the setting, and in particular, the metaphors used in communication. A metaphor is a figure of speech, an analogy that links the current setting or situation to another one that bears some symbolic and logical similarities. A metaphor, however, evokes in the mind of the listener (or reader) many aspects of the other entity. For example, when someone says, "This school is a prison," the listener might well conclude that the teachers are like wardens, that the students are regimented, that students are there against their will, and so forth. Dominant metaphors shape thinking by generating a range of taken-for-granted assumptions.

Metaphors that dominate contemporary thinking about schools are the military, industrial and business models (highly bureaucratic, or course), and athletics. House and Mitchell (1974) demonstrated the prevalence of the military-industrial metaphor in the language of a widely used textbook on supervision. The sports metaphor is evident in that many school administrators are former coaches. The team coach is often seen as the appropriate person to head an education organization. Coaching and teaching appear in the leadership and staff development literature as being significantly linked as an organizational leadership style. The team concept permeates the literature in areas such as team building, school-based management, participatory management, problem-solving teams, and so on.

But, as in the bureaucratic metaphor, these other metaphors may undermine effective problem solving because they imply nonreflective behavior styles. The good athlete, soldier, or worker follows orders, acts promptly and reflexively, requires physical training, and seeks to win or beat the competition at all costs. Intermediate and tangible results are the norm in military, industrial, political, and athletic organizations; long-range outcomes are scarcely considered, and team mediocrity is often preferred to individual creativity.

The prevailing bureaucratic model and the dominant metaphors of military-industrial behavior and athletics are at odds with effective problem analysis based on professional values. Hold the traditional metaphors and attendant constraints in abeyance while learning and practicing some new ways of thinking and some effective problem-solving techniques. The introduction of the "problem of the solution" opens new problems or creates a new set of flaws for problem analysis. When principals engage in analysis and decision making concerning students, teachers, and other stakeholders at the school, a solution may lead to a totally different set of circumstances, discoveries, analyses, decisions, and problems.

Whatever else organizations may be—problem-solving instruments, sociological structures, reward systems, and so on—they are political entities. Organizations operate by distributing authority, status, and other rewards and by setting a stage for the exercise of influence, if not of power. Is it any wonder, therefore, that individuals who are highly motivated to secure and use power find a familiar and hospitable environment in public education administration? The challenge is to use that power well.

To be successful in organizational life, a person must understand organizations and the organizations' functions and roles in the larger scheme of things as well as the functions and roles of the positions within the organizations. Whether consciously or not, people successful in organization life understand something of the theory and of the attendant sociological/psychological factors of groups, systems, and individuals. To function in this maze of complexity, a person must come equipped with some basis of understanding how all of these factors impact on one another, or as is more likely the case, the person learns about organizational life through a combination of experience and study. More and more, there is concern for the stewardship role of organizations for the clients they serve. Total quality refers to the organization's sensitivity levels and to its clients as well as to quality products.

Stakeholders associated with the school should be involved when and where appropriate in the continuum of problem analysis, especially in helping determine likely causes of the problem and in conducting any required information searches. Education's concerned stakeholders include parents, students, teachers, administrators, government—in general, the citizenry at large. In his work with parenting and parent involvement, Lueder (1997) has found that as educators work toward likely problem causes and solutions in education, support from parents is a key part of their addressing and solving the developmental problems in schools and schooling.

Visioning and problem finding are traits of effective principals, and these traits are found in effective administrators in whatever fields of work they may find themselves (Peterson, 1986). Successful administrators use vision to guide their organizations to high levels of achievement. Visioning helps a person make a distinction between, or at least to recognize the discrepancy between, *what is* (empirical) and some preferred state often called *what ought to be* (normative) (Reynolds and Silver, 1987).

SEEK THE PROBLEM OF THE SOLUTION

After sorting out "the problem of the problem," the "problem of the solution" takes center stage. Problem analysis continues after the problem is put into a definitive form so that the problem analyst can then seek a reasonable solution, *the problem of the solution.*

Suppose that a faculty member said to you, "We have a communication problem among our faculty. What would you suggest we do about it?" You undoubtedly want to ask many questions and seek additional information before hazarding an action suggestion. What is not being communicated? Who feels the need for such communication? Why isn't this communication taking place? Who would need to be communicating what to whom to improve the problem situation? What is the perception of what is being expressed?

At one level, the problem of the solution suggests that when a solution to one problem is *REACHED*, another problem is *CREATED*; each solution may be its own problem. In some cases a solution could create a larger, more complex problem than the original problem or situation. This gives rise to the notion that sometimes the original problem might be better left alone.

Part of the problem of the solution is the task of categorizing a proposed solution into degrees of complexity where a solution might become more of a problem than doing little or nothing about the problem. The problem analyzer might consider (1) the *value* of the solution versus new problems that the solution is likely to create, (2) who is *really* affected most by the solution, and (3) that the solution may be more *harmful* than the problem, that is, a solution may add a burden to someone outside of the problem situation.

In the first category of value would be the simple solution that calls only for an explanation or some type of minor regulatory response. If a student breaks a bus rule, the student is suspended from bus privileges. The problem brought about by this solution is likely to be threefold: (1) the student will have to find other acceptable transportation, (2) this task may fall to the parents and require them to adjust their schedules, or (3) the student will be absent. The problem that the solution may cause has to be balanced between the lesson learned by the student (the example taught) and the hardship on student and parents.

In the second category of who is really affected, consider who is affected most in a proposed solution. Is the solution appropriate to the problem, and are the consequences focused on the right person or persons, purpose, or lesson? It may be right to ask what is the greater purpose served in this solution. Consider this scenario. A student is aware that his father, a teacher in the school, is having an affair with another married teacher in the school. The female teacher also has a son, and the two young men are close friends. One day the young men get into a fight in school over their parents' affair. The school rule is that they both are to be suspended for 3 days for fighting. The parents must then meet with the principal. The solution seems simple: Just apply the rule! However, other circumstances have to be considered. What about the parents? Will the whole thing explode? The choice is not as simple as it first seems and may trigger other problems, perhaps some even greater than the fighting. What choice should be made in this situation?

In the third category of harmful, the solution may be no action, or that things are better left alone because the consequences could be overwhelming. But, in this situation the principal might want to inform his or her superior of the decision. Perhaps the principal believes, or even "knows" that someone is guilty of breaking a rule but cannot prove it to the degree that would bring a preferred solution to a successful conclusion. In other words, if a principal "knows" something to be true, but cannot prove it beyond a shadow of a doubt, to proceed at this point might be unwise. (Knowledge and proof are not always the same.) Maturity of judgment and a willingness and persistence in searching for additional information are key. Perhaps "murder will out," or, if given enough rope the person will "hang himself." This condition is especially true with young people who must tell about their exploits to gain peer recognition.

CATEGORIZING PROBLEMS

In moving from problem identification and problem framing or categorizing, to decisions and action (and, of course, to the new problems caused by the preferred solution), consider the "flow" of problem analysis (see Figure 3.1).

FIGURE 3.1. FLOW OF ACTION IN PROBLEM ANALYSIS FROM INITIAL PROBLEM FINDING OR IDENTIFICATION TO THE CONDITIONS FOR A NEW PROBLEM

Problem   Problem   Problem   Problem
Finding ➜ Categorizing ➜Disposition ➜   Solutions
                                              ↓

                                   Action & Change
                                          ↓

                                   New Problems

(➜ = *leading to*)

Problems requiring action run the continuum from high-stakes to low-stakes decisions, with a time (priority or urgency) base from high to low. For example, a problem could be classified as low priority and low risk, high priority and low risk, and so on (see Figure 3.2). In seeking solutions, the principal should analyze the situation in accordance with the model suggested in Figure 3.2 to help sort out forces that influence the potential decision(s) made regarding placing priorities on problems. The matrix in Figure 3.2 shows four options for considering factors impinging on the problem of the problem. Quadrant 1 is pressure-packed, whereas quadrant 4 is relatively calm.

After considering the factors of risk and priority, the principal would act on problems in the same four general categories.

FIGURE 3.2. A CLASSIFICATION OF FACTORS INFLUENCING THE PRESSURES GENERATED BY PROBLEMS

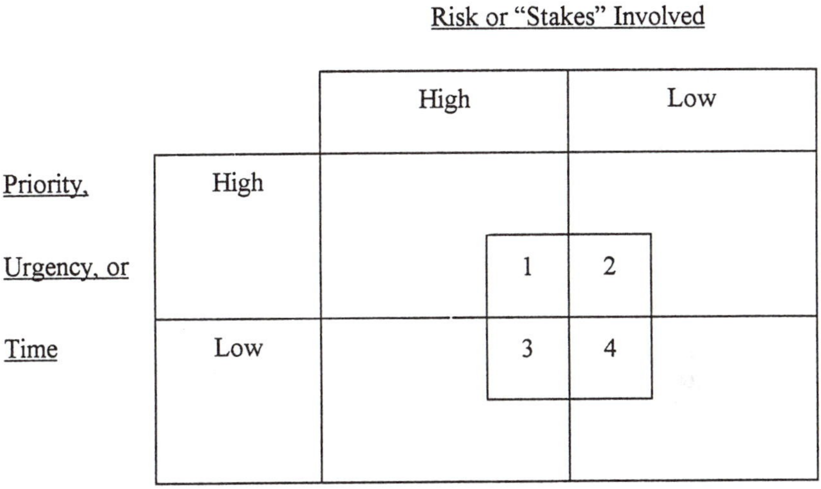

Risk or "Stakes" Involved

		High	Low
Priority,	High		
Urgency, or		1	2
Time	Low	3	4

There is, however, a fifth action alternative not totally available in the classifications shown in Figure 3.2; that option is to decide to do nothing. A do-nothing problem could be so low stakes and low priority that it is simply too trivial to bother with. If so, it is a quadrant 4 problem. There are other do-nothing settings. The do-nothing alternative may arise after careful problem analysis. The do-nothing decision may occur through inattention to problem analysis or because of ignorance. Choosing the do-nothing alternative should come after careful problem analysis.

DO NOTHING

The do-nothing option may be a viable alternative in some settings. Under certain circumstances problems are best left alone. In the do-nothing case, the risk factor comes from the possible consequences associated with doing nothing. If some higher good is served by doing nothing, then pleading ignorance might be the best problem analysis. Gray's line in "Ode to the Distant Prospect of Eton College" states the sentiment poetically: "When ignorance is bliss, 'tis folly to be wise"; however, if ignorance is simple avoidance behavior for self-serving reasons, consequences and risk could be great. One key to deciding to do nothing will be what serves the greater purpose. Sometimes a large-scale analysis other than introspection and reflection may bring unneeded attention to the problem. For example, when a person tells you in confidence something that you know in all likelihood is not true, you assuredly maintain the confidence!

♦ A woman comes up the walk outside your office window. You know that she is coming to rehash a trivial matter. You have a serious problem to solve that requires your immediate attention and you are in a bad mood. You exit quickly out the back.

The do-nothing solution serves a higher good of avoiding an unnecessary conflict while affording time to solve more pressing problems. This situation might also be considered a low priority/low risk problem with a "no action" solution.

LOW PRIORITY/LOW RISK

A low priority, low risk problem may be "put on the back burner" or passed on to others for solution and action. This situation could serve as a training opportunity for others, but sensitivity, awareness, consequences, and complementary associations are important considerations. The NASSP Assessment Centers and other in-basket training/simulation programs address decision-making and delegation skills. Low priority/low risk problems can offer opportunities for practice without punishment, or practice without fear of failure in problem solving/problem analysis activities. A low priority/low risk problem might be a note from the superintendent asking for an explanation of a discrepancy in the athletic budget where some funds were transferred from one account to another without sufficient notation. If solving this routine posting error can be assigned to a bookkeeper or to the athletic director, this action gives the person to whom the task is assigned responsibility for communication and for being accountable. This action also places the problem at its origin for determination; it contributes to the shared decision-making process of school based-management (SBM) and trains those who deal with these decisions so that the problems won't recur.

♦ Your school has been allocated money for purchase of materials. How should you distribute those funds with fairness and equity? You can feel comfortable in delegating this process to others to gain goodwill, trust, loyalty, and to help develop responsible and accountable associates. You may ask to have the results presented to you before they are widely made known.

HIGH PRIORITY/LOW RISK

High priority/low risk problems can be addressed directly or can be delegated in accordance with the need and area concerned. For example, a student's parents are in the superintendent's office waiting for a response concerning disciplinary action taken against their child. They believe that this action was arbitrary. The superintendent wants a review of the situation by the end of the day as a basis for a response to the parents. If this routine request from the superintendent needs a quick answer, the principal might assign at least responsibility for information gathering and response to another staff person. However, if the principal senses complications in the process or outcome the principal may choose a different tack. Complications in the situation might change the problem to a high priority/high risk condition. The principal may consider this normally low-risk matter as a high-risk situation because of the superintendent's involvement. In this case, the priority remains high but not as important as the risk if the wrong move is made in response. Is the superintendent making an improper intervention by not sending the parents back to the school? This action points out the importance of having a sensitivity for the circumstances and an awareness of the existing conditions.

♦ A policy exempts seniors who have an average of B or better from taking final exams. A junior who has an A average in a class usually taken only by seniors wishes to be exempted too. You deny the request. The student calls the school board chairperson. The next morning before the exam you are told that the school board chairperson said that the student should be exempt.

LOW PRIORITY/HIGH RISK

A low priority/high risk situation is usually perplexing. Even though the problem is not high priority, it could become high risk if it is not handled correctly. For example, the superintendent asked to receive from you a copy of the policy on building rentals by a certain date so that the policy could be presented to the County Commissioners as part of a new cooperative planning endeavor. You had 10 days to send it. At the time it was not a high priority. That was 10 days ago; you forgot and did not send it. The message that you are inadvertently sending could be that the superintendent's request was not important to you. This is a bad message! Worse, this policy is an important agenda item at the joint School Board and County Commissioners meeting later today.

HIGH PRIORITY/HIGH RISK

The high priority/high risk situation probably will need the principal's acknowledgment, stamp of approval, and attention throughout the whole process. This situation will require a quick and decisive response and the consequences will be important, for example, to the safety, security, growth, and so on, of all concerned. Consider the following. A father greets the principal at 7:05 a.m. at the school saying that a black male student has been harassing his white female daughter, and he wants the principal to do something now or he will go to the local newspaper and police department. The principal should recognize that this problem has immediate and long-range consequences. If it is handled improperly, the risk could multiply exponentially. One problem-resolution strategy could be to seek help with the problem from a higher authority or to involve someone better prepared to address the problem. This situation could involve the whole district and community, so at a minimum the superintendent should be notified immediately. This might require a legal decision that would involve the school attorney.

THE PROBLEM STATEMENT

A good problem statement is a brief, specific representation of a problem situation, perhaps even in the form of a well-defined question. A problem situation exists when there is a difference between the way things are perceived to be and the way that someone would like them to be (discrepancy). Unfortunately the word *problem* carries a negative connotation for many people. The discrepancy distinction, however, can be applied in good situations; that is, an accomplishment of a new objective could make a situation even better. For example, your commodious minivan satisfies your family's basic transportation needs, but you believe that having a compact car, too, would make things even better in terms of gas mileage, convenience, and so on. There is no negative connotation here, but there is an expression of a desire for change.

Using the definition of a problem situation as one where there is a discrepancy between the way things are perceived now and the way someone would like them to be assures that there are always problems to be worked on. The more fertile a person's mind is for conjuring up better conditions, the greater the store of problems available to challenge the range of solutions. There are always improvement goals that energetic and successful administrators will be working toward. One great barrier to working constructively toward achieving improvement goals is a lack of specificity and clarity in stating the problem. Compare two efforts to state the same problem.

1. "We have a communication problem among our faculty."

2. "We use team teaching in our building. Virtually all of us involved in teams are concerned that we haven't given adequate attention to creating ways to share innovative ideas across teams. We need ways of sharing that don't take up the time of people to whom a particular idea is not relevant but that do convey enough detail for interested parties to know how to use the idea in their own settings."

Although the second problem representation is longer than the first, the added detail structures the setting so that the solution steps are likely to be more thorough and successful. The second problem representation includes four elements that express the problem in a format that gives direction for action.

FOUR GUIDELINE QUESTIONS TO HELP STRUCTURE PROBLEMS

These four questions give structure to the processes in problem solving. The examples are from the problem statements above.

- **Who is affected?** Members of the teaching teams are affected. "Virtually all of us involved in teams are concerned...."

- **Who (or what) seems to cause it?** The members of the teaching teams seem to see themselves as mainly responsible. "...We haven't given adequate attention...."

- **What kind of problem is it?** Note that the teachers see the reason for the problem as a lack of adequate means for doing something else. "We need ways of sharing...." The reason could be a lack of knowledge.

- **What is the goal for improvement?** Specifically, how will things look when the goal has been achieved? The goal is not simply increased communication. The goal is creating "...ways of sharing that don't take up time of people to whom a particular idea is not relevant, but that do convey enough detail for interested parties to know how to use the idea in their settings."

A good problem statement will include an improvement goal. Clarity is important because there may be several possible and plausible major and minor goals in the problem situation. When describing the problem situation, answer the four guideline questions but also focus clearly on one specific improvement goal. As you solve a problem, other improvement goals may emerge, and new problems may become evident.

Confusion may arise from being specific in expressing the problem statement while also being flexible enough to change the statement whenever new understandings of the problem occur. In the early stages of working on a problem, people may have quite different ideas about the problem and what the improvement goal should be. Stating the presumed cause and goal specifically gives direction to the next problem analysis steps (e.g., refining and reframing the original problem). The clearer the initial problem statement, the more likely that the principal will improve on the initial analysis whenever new information unfolds. *The problem statement should be as specific as possible, but always open for change in the light of new data and understandings.*

CLARIFYING RESPONSES TO INITIAL PROBLEM ANALYSES

In responding to the four guideline questions for expressing a problem statement, be as specific as possible. The prior four guideline questions are expanded here with sample probing questions that can assist in the analysis of a problem situation.

- ♦ **Who is affected?** Consider all possibilities carefully before proceeding. Does the problem affect only you? One other person? A small group of people? An entire organization? The community at large?

- ♦ **Who or what is causing the problem or problem situation?** We frequently speak of problems as though they were caused by circumstances that don't relate directly to people. This is almost never the case. Bureaucratic language and passive voice perpetuate this spurious thinking. *Shun the "It just happened" fallacy* as exemplified by, "It is believed that...." Someone believes. Almost always some person or persons are at the heart of things. Consider the same possibilities as above. Is it you? One other person? A small group of people? An entire organization? Is it the community or society at large?

- ♦ **What kind of problem is it?** There are many ways to think about kinds of problems. The definition of the problem often helps set the directions that solutions may take. Consider for analysis the following possibilities for problem situations:

  - Disagreement or a lack of clarity about goals. (Goal or Purpose Problem)

  - A lack of clarity or a disagreement about the means of achieving goals. (Process Problem)

- A lack of skills needed to carry out a particular means or a lack of material resources. (Instrumental Problem)

- Inaccurate communication or too little or too much communication. People have different understandings of the same thing. (Communication Problem)

- Insufficient time or conflicting schedules. (Time Problem)

- Inappropriate roles or restrictive, unclear norms. (Structure Problem)

- Conflicting ideologies. (Beliefs and Values Problem)

- Lack of clarity or a conflict about turf issues, rewards or decision-making prerogatives. (Power Struggle Problem)

- Individual differences or sensitivity issues. (Personnel/Personality Problem)

- A lack of knowledge that is not likely to be adjusted easily by training. (Competence Problem)

♦ **Solution Criteria: What are the goals for improvement?** Ideally, the criteria for a successful problem solution should be stated so clearly that anyone hearing the problem statement would know how to determine when the goal had been reached. Solution criteria indicate exactly who would be doing what, where, when, how, and to what extent. Without a road map for getting to the heart of the problem, it's difficult to make and execute plans to get there. One irony is that the more clearly and precisely you state the intended target, the more likely you are to recognize that it could be an incorrect target.

THE IDENTIFIED PROBLEM IS THE PROBLEM

What parts of analysis follow after you determine that the identified problem IS the problem that you will work on? Problem analysis now begins to address the is-ought discrepancy to increase the likelihood of a successful solution (Reynolds and Silver, 1987). A second irony is the idea that the solution to the first problem will be a problem too! This might be termed "The Problems Because of The Solution."

The main areas of discussion in the following sections are likely causes of the problem and information search. In these discussions, assume that "The Problem" has been identified correctly. No problem can really be solved until someone finds and analyzes its causes. Unfortunately, many people use a "ready, fire, aim" approach to problem analysis and solving (Segal and Meyers, 1988). Finding and analyzing problem causes requires a process that begins with a clear description of the conditions (and perhaps the context) and ends with a definite plan of action.

Segal and Meyers (1988) designed a model for "taking aim" at problems.

♦ Address the questions of who, what, where, when, how much.

♦ Identify "killer causes." Identify as many causes as possible and then synthesize all of those to a few (the "killer causes").

♦ Brainstorm possible solutions, analyzing one "killer cause" at a time. The key is to analyze the "workability" of all possible solutions.

♦ Choose the preferred solution.

♦ Apply the preferred solution.

♦ Determine one or more back-up plans or alternatives.

This model also calls for an organizational philosophy that requires participatory problem analysis—a team effort, or, as we call it, *complementary associations*.

The consideration of time comes to bear on the "identification of likely causes" and, therefore, impacts on the problem of the solution (Segal and Meyers, 1988). In recent works Leithwood (1995), Keedy (1995, personal communication), and others distinguish between the problem-handling abilities of the expert and of the nonexpert principal. One main difference is experience in handling problems. Experienced principals will consider time an important factor in dealing with causes, whereas inexperienced principals often look for immediate solutions, thereby skipping both careful analysis of probable causes and detailed information search. New principals are often caught up in power struggles and cannot see the need for reflection or search, so they believe that they cannot take the time for detailed problem analysis. The expert principal will also determine where the problem falls in the matrix that addresses priority and risk (Figure 3.2, p. 63). Consider this example of priority, risk, and experience.

♦ You have a serious heart condition and need open-heart surgery. Many surgeons have read about how to do open-heart surgery. Some have studied books written by surgeons famous for successful open-heart surgery. Some may have assisted in such surgery. Nevertheless, you will select a physician with considerable successful experience in open-heart surgery rather than choose a person new to the field. Why? Experience. Another reason, perhaps less obvious, is that you "feel" that persons who have successful experience doing such surgery would know what to do if something should go wrong. That is, you understand that their experiences have given them a knowledge beyond the basic procedures of the surgery, a knowledge that they could use if a problem should arise. When *your* life is on the line, you will bet on experience.

In the literature on problem analysis, two findings seem especially noteworthy. The first, as reported in Leithwood and Steinbach (1995, p. 41), is that when compared to novices, experts in problem analysis use "more abstract categories (as opposed to more superficial features of the problem) with reference to more basic principles (Berliner, 1986)"; second, experts "have better and faster pattern-recognition skills (Bereiter and Scardamalia, 1986)." That is, experts more than nonexperts are quicker in recognizing and using similarities/differences between the current problem situation and other situations.

Moore (1990) posed the conundrum that if we accept that experience aids in the ability to formulate problems successfully, can behaviors acquired through experience be taught? Fredericksen (1984) suggested that we know little about teaching people to develop representations of ill-structured problems, to develop plans for solving such problems, or to employ appropriate strategies or heuristic approaches. Perhaps there are processes and heuristics that we can learn from experience and that we can teach, or perhaps those processes and techniques must be individually discovered. In either case, an approach to problematic educational situations for novices could be identified so that such processes and heuristics might be discovered more easily. As a surrogate for actual experience, learning of these skills may be facilitated through careful use of case studies, problem-based learning exercises, simulation and role playing, and problem-centered internships.

Keedy (1995, personal communication) summarized some elements of differences between expert and nonexpert principals in regard to problem solving. He reported that, "Using this abstraction, the principal decided what should get his immediate attention; the abstraction provided a structure for problem solving" (p. 3).

Leithwood and Stager (1989) compared expert with nonexpert principals on problem-solving efforts. Particularly in dealing with unstructured as opposed to structured problems, these researchers found that:

- ♦ Expert principals knew how to solve problems. They recognized various problems and patterns from experience and therefore solutions were familiar (p. 140).

- ♦ Experts in problem solving tended to be very explicit about their assumptions regarding the hypothetical nature of problems presented to them (p. 141).

- ♦ Regarding goal-setting, the experts were better able to see the implications of problems not directly concerned with students and programs (p. 144).

- ♦ Experts applied more principles to their problem solutions (long-term goals grounded in fundamental laws, doctrines, assumptions). For example, regarding his entry as a principal in a school, one expert suggested, "If the kids are turned off, they will start to look for things to criticize" (p. 146).

IDENTIFICATION OF LIKELY CAUSES

Upon becoming aware of a problem situation, some administrators jump immediately into action. This hasty behavior could be a serious blunder that might address only symptoms. A more thoughtful administrator might deliberate appropriate action that resolves underlying problem causes. Of the several steps that might intervene between problem awareness and problem solution, *identification of likely problem causes* is arguably the most important and the approach applied separates an expert from a novice. Identification of likely causes is a difficult step for principals who believe that prompt action is the mark of an effective leader and that hesitancy is a sign of weakness and indecisiveness. Unfortunately, when time is not a major variable, a rush to action might be a sign of inexperience or immaturity. Identification of likely causes sometimes requires postponing action to reflect upon the meaning of a given situation. The importance of identifying likely causes of problems is provided in detail later, but the following four points summarize the key steps.

Searching beyond the obvious, immediate causes for more basic causes. Looking beyond the obvious involves such things as probing for other people's motives or interests and searching for dysfunctional institutional patterns. This takes skill, training , and good sense. As the problem scenario is examined, stories often get changed as they get retold. Sometimes people explain things that get misinterpreted through translation, retranslation, or distance from the original source ("he said/she said"). In searching for origins, the "eye witness" may clear up some mystery surrounding the problem. Reframing situations can be helpful. Look at situations through the eyes of others. Imagine different scenarios and situations and follow trails. Look within the following vignettes for possible problem causes:

- ◆ A student comes into the principal's office and accuses his teacher of calling him a "nerd" in front of the class. The student is obviously distressed and very upset with the teacher. *What might be some of the possible causes of this problem?*
  - Student is a "wimp" or "nerd."
  - Teacher is in a bad frame of mind, physically ill, or tired.

- Teacher is insecure so the teacher puts others down.
- Student has had a personality conflict with teacher all year.
- Teacher's mate just left home.
- Teacher is angry with the student because the student would not cooperate.
- Teacher was teasing and did not intend to offend the student.

Any of these (or many other examples) could be a cause of the altercation. In addressing this and the following situations, the expert principal will consider such things as discrepancy, priority, risk, time factor, and expectation or vision of harmony. What are some possible causes in the following vignettes? Where would you go to find information that might be relevant? How might you determine possible causes?

♦ A teacher has sent a note to the principal stating that a neighboring teacher cannot seem to control her class.

♦ A teacher recently made some dramatic changes in his or her style of dress and you hear that questions are being asked among teachers and students.

Using behavioral science knowledge to understand social dynamics. Whatever theories you know (and can learn) about psychology, sociology, anthropology, political science, or economics can be used to enrich your understanding of the underlying dynamics of the problem situation. Being a people watcher and understanding, or at least being sensitive to, nonverbal communication can be a useful skill in recognizing and analyzing probable causes. The nonverbal sense is even more important now than in the past as we become more of a multicultural society. Framing problems and their solutions in cultural contexts also should be a consideration.

♦ The football coach comes to your office and complains that a 12th grade English teacher, who is also the English department chairperson, has decreed that athletes (football players) will not be released early under any circumstances.

♦ A principal of a large (3,000 students) high school in a relatively small southern town is confronted with information about "a problem" by a local businessman who is also a good friend. The "problem," according to the businessman, is that a black teacher's aide at your school is dating a white student.

Recognizing intraschool causes of problems. Whereas a "natural" tendency is to attribute causes of problems to external factors or some amorphous "them" (such as another individual's personality or motives, budget limits, home environment, or legal constraints), recognizing that many problem causes lie *within* the school provides the principal with opportunities for constructive action. This idea is embedded in Pogo's celebrated dictum, "We have encountered the enemy and it is us!" Teachers may contribute to problems because of their lack of patience and understanding. Personality conflicts may add to problem situations when teachers do not realize how many different ways they may communicate negativism to others.

Introspection, self-analysis, and self-critique. Difficult aspects of searching for likely problem causes for principals are the introspection, self-analysis, and self-critique needed to discover how they themselves may have instigated or exacerbated the situation. The principal may find that she or he is the problem! This can be determined by introspection: "How might I have influenced this situation?" Getting honest feedback from other people, which may be a difficult condition for any leader, is a necessary step toward a solution. To complete the material in Appendix A, the principal must consider school-based and self-based possible causes of a problem. The Case Record process (Silver, 1984 and 1987; Osterman, 1991) can be used both to help define a problem clearly and to guide successful problem solving. Use the Case Record form and study a problem at your work site (Appendix A).

♦ You are the principal of a 1,500-student high school with a 20% minority population. You have completed the written evaluations of the staff and have presented them to individual staff members for their review. It is 3:45 P.M. on Thursday afternoon and Ms. Smith, a black teacher, has entered your office and confronted you by saying that your evaluation of her is prejudiced on two counts: first, she is black and second, she is female! She asks that you give her a response no later than the following afternoon. *Assume the role of the principal. List your initial estimate of the possible causes contributing to this accusation. Where would you go for information? What would be your first step? What do you think is the problem?*

SEARCHING FOR RELEVANT INFORMATION

Another part of "the Problem of the Solution" is "searching for relevant information." The NPBEA (Thomson, 1993) suggested that a principal's behavior in gathering, categorizing, sifting, and synthesizing information might be as follows. First, categorize information by source. Next, classify it according to credibility, reliability, and validity. In working through this process, determine the factors of time, risk, and priority. If there is time, consult with expert sources concerning such things as legal and medical matters, if needed. In reflecting on the situation, look at the information pool for logic and sequencing of events. Hold in abeyance or discard useless and irrelevant information.

♦ It is rumored that interracial dating is going on among students in your school and a school board member wants you to check on this.

♦ A parent calls and tells you about a party that is supposed to be held Saturday night. Students from your school will be attending. This parent indicates that alcohol and drugs will be present.

How would you begin to gather appropriate information in these situations? Are these "problems" yours to solve?

VALIDITY AND RELIABILITY IN PROBLEM-ANALYSIS STEPS

A principal needs to analyze information and sources of information to determine whether they are credible. Credibility usually is determined by such things as knowing the environment, culture, condition, and source of information. Knowing the source of information and that source's past performance helps the principal. If the information comes from a source that has established credibility and accuracy over a period of time, then it may be considered valid and reliable. One problem confounding the "problem of the solution" can be a change of sources, and a principal discovers that credibility is then questionable. For example, a process always followed under certain circumstances is altered after a change in upper-level administration. The credibility of the old process becomes questionable, and new processes and norms must be applied and tested for their own credibility. If credibility is not reestablished, anxiety, distrust, and so on, may become a problem.

- Kelly Whitcomb is the chorus director. The chorus is on a trip to perform in another community. At the motel where the chorus is staying, two students leave with an unknown third party and go to a store where they purchase liquor, which several students drink in their rooms later. The chaperone was apparently unaware of the situation. Word gets back to the principal on Monday afternoon through "the grapevine." *What needs to be included in an information search in this vignette? Who is responsible? What can be done to see that this does not occur again? What are some time factors involved?*

- A school board member is pressuring principals to address the issue of tracking by reducing the number of levels (tracks) in the curriculum.

- A teacher just told you that she heard at a local bridge club that your AP English teacher is moonlighting at a nightclub in a neighboring town as an exotic dancer. *List some key questions that need to be processed. Compare your questions with a colleague. Where does the information search begin on these problems? Should the principal even be concerned with these?*

During the information search for this last problem situation, the principal might consider reviewing the teacher's background, the people who have a personal impact on the teacher's life, the people vicariously involved (bridge club), and so on. What are possible sources of information? What are possible causes? What is the time element involved? Do you go to see the "show"? Would conditions change if the teacher were moonlighting as an *erotic* dancer? What are the validity and reliability concerns?

In this age of technology, information search can take on new perspectives through the information highway and the many networking possibilities. Computer and electronic library services provide expanded ways to search for and gather information. Although electronic networks provide quick access to volumes of information, human contacts, connections, intuitiveness, processes, and flexibility are still central in information search. Most problems that a professional must deal with are interpersonal and intrapersonal, but problem analysis is not confined to "people problems." The problem of the solution runs the continuum from the abstract to the concrete. Sometimes person-to-person is the only way to resolve a "people problem" satisfactorily.

STRUCTURED AND UNSTRUCTURED PROBLEMS

The NPBEA Problem Analysis discussion suggested that problems can be placed into two basic categories: structured and unstructured (Thomson, 1993). A structured problem is routine and an unstructured problem requires more time, analysis, and reflection. (See the discussion in Chapter 2.) Time is a major consideration in crises responses. An opportunity-related problem allows more time and flexibility. Revisit some prior vignettes to determine if they allow the administrator enough time to be flexible in seeking problem causes. Flexibility increases when a decision is not needed immediately, and the principal has time to reframe, reflect, reconstruct, and gather added information to improve the possibility of better solutions.

How to expand the information base is a learning process and each problem analysis can add to the principal's memory bank. Using information search for professional growth is an opportunity-related problem. Reflecting on the possibilities inherent in each new problem is a professional growth opportunity. An administrator may react to a situation in an aura of arrogance or without enough information, believing that his or her way is right, and not seek opportunities for growth in the solving of each problem. Buying time is a calculated strategy in problem analysis. If reflection is important, then stepping back from a situation to gain time for reflection can be a good strategy.

In the earlier vignette where the AP English teacher is reported to be moonlighting, the principal should consider several questions. How much time exists to gather the necessary information? What are the contingencies involved? The information could be hearsay, second hand, jealousy, rumor, or even totally without substance. Who can provide more information? Are there legal issues here? Should the principal inform superiors of the rumor? When does the principal talk to the teacher? Are due process procedures important? Does it even matter? These many contingencies suggest the need for buying time to conduct a careful information search.

Some studies reported by Leithwood and Steinbach (1995) show that more experienced problem solvers consider new and different factors in searching for causes, in information gathering, and in subsequent reflection and decision-making than do less experienced ones. Keedy (1995) reported that wizened principals who have developed personal theories of practice make better decisions on routine matters than do new or less experienced principals. Literature and research also suggest that a principal's theories of practice can be adaptable and become tools of the trade. The application of general theories is tempered by the context, situation, and the individual's personality makeup. Certain steps may be predictable, but specific applications depend on circumstances and the individual's personality, and may vary over time. The experienced administrator, like "The Gambler" in Kenny Roger's song, is a person who knows "when to hold them and when to fold them."

Today's educational administrators live in a turbulent world of rapids, shoals, and "white water." (Vail, 1989, as cited by Leithwood, Steinbach, and Raun, 1993, p. 364.) This is "a world in which few assumptions are beyond scrutiny and the environment sometimes appears chaotic." Yet, in spite of the rapids, shoals, and whirlpools, the principal's desk is where the "buck stops" in the school building. People expect the principal to create calm from chaos. Problem analysis and its components—problem finding, problem solving, decision-making, and change—are parts of administration no matter in what task the person is involved. The outcome (the [?] in the model below) needs to be evaluated as one way to improve problem analysis.

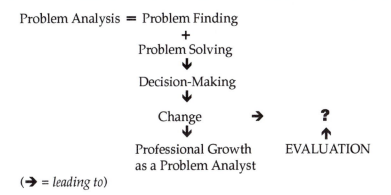

($\rightarrow$ = *leading to*)

SOME MODELS FOR PROBLEM SOLVING

♦ A principal who has worked for years to become "in charge" of a school suddenly realizes that she or he is not "really" in charge. Times, people, and parent involvement have changed. There are local site councils and even union demands. The new principal reflects...

This realization may generate frustration and problems if the person does not develop an awareness of and sensitivity to the position and to the organizational culture. In years past, those being led generally accepted the exercise of power by "the boss." This is no longer the case. Power has been diffused by the many social movements of the past 50 years and people generally are better educated. History books remind readers that emblazoned on flags of the independent colonies during the early growth of our country was the phrase, "Don't Tread on Me," indicating individual state's rights and harsh reckoning if the warning went unheeded. Early public schools can be likened to the old states' rights, though they never flew "Don't Tread on Me" battle flags. The prevailing attitude until the late 1950s was to leave the school business to "the professionals."

Today, everyone wants a piece of the action known as education. Public education is one government function within easy reach of a frustrated voting public, and public education takes a large proportion of tax dollars, mostly from people who do not have school-aged children. People may feel that institutions and organizations are suffering from "fatal learning disabilities" (Senge, 1990), and show distrust of education in the push toward home schooling, charter schools, vouchers, or other types of privatization. Senge spoke about teamwork and developing a systematic process to address the issues confronting modern organizations, including education. He argued that a systems application using a high level of awareness is the modern mode of functioning for "learning organizations." "The organizations that will excel in the future will be the organizations that discover how to tap people's commitment and capacity to learn at all levels in an organization" (p. 4). Translated to education, and more specifically to problem analysis, Senge's concepts argue that a systematic process should be applied to problem analysis.

The literature presents models for problem analysis and the models have striking similarities. Figures 3.3 through 3.5 (pp. 84–85) show three such models. Figure 3.3, developed in 1987 by Reynolds and Silver (and expanded by McWhirt, Reynolds, and Achilles, 1989), begins with problem awareness and problem finding. This process model consists of eight steps. The two other models, one outlined by NPBEA (Thomson, 1993) (Figure 3.4) and one developed by Schmuck and Schmuck (1983) (Figure 3.5), show considerable similarities in approaches to problem analysis. This agreement among models is one reality check, a validity step, by which to judge the problem-solving process.

Although we present some processes and models for problem solving and display those in Figures 3.3 through 3.5, we recognize the potential danger of providing models as readers might believe that there is a formula for problem analysis. The works reported by Leithwood and Steinbach (1995) and by Hallinger, Leithwood, and Murphy (1993) showed clearly that knowledge and experience contribute to expert problem analysis, but that there is no formula either for problem defining or for problem solving. If the complex problems of principals allowed the application of mechanical solutions to routine, structured, presented, or academic problems with a known method of solution and a known answer (e.g., if the side of a square is 2 feet, what is its area?), a book on problem analysis might include formulas and a manual of solutions. The method and answers (e.g., 2 feet × 2 feet = 4 square feet) are not known in complex, nonroutine, and discovered problems common in a principal's work. For example, two name callings, and two "A said/B said" episodes do not always equal counseling, or peer mediation, or parental conferences. Figures 2.3, 2.4, and 2.5 (pp. 43–45) in Chapter 2 portray some of the differences between routine or presented problems and discovered or nonroutine problems. These differences suggest the difficulties one would have in trying to apply a formula for problem analysis.

However, to help the reader employ a structured problem analysis process, we have provided an example in Appendix B of using the framework in Figure 3.3 as a guide to problem analysis. The reader may wish to review the explanation of the models in Figures 3.3, 3.4, and 3.5 briefly, and then turn to Appendix B to see the application of the model. The eight-step model in Figuree 3.3 developed by Reynolds and Silver (1987) is explained in the fairly detailed description below.

AWARENESS OF PROBLEM SITUATION

Some administrators may never reach a conscious awareness of the problem, or of the act of problem finding. A leader needs a level of awareness that transcends the routine or mundane. This person must develop high levels of sensitivity and perceptiveness. The successful principal will seek and identify problems so that clear and important solutions become possible. Being aware that something is amiss, that there is a flaw or imperfection, is an essential precondition for making improvements. (McWhirt, Reynolds, and Achilles, 1989).

Once aware that something is amiss, the problem analyzer can begin looking at the problem in reference to the ideal state or preferred state. For example, an outstanding teacher is having marital problems that are affecting work at school. In the ideal state, this situation is resolved with all parties happy and functional. The process of analyzing and solving the problem is focused on that ideal state (Vision).

Reframing suggests changing perspective, reversing, looking at a problem from a different angle, with a change of place, or change of players, and so on. This might address the question, "What if...?" For example, in the case of the teacher with marital problems, in a conservative environment one vision of the ideal might be to try to patch up the relationship so they would live happily ever after. Yet, other themes are possible. After considering likely scenarios, the principal might encourage the couple to seek other alternatives to get on with their lives. Here, reframing is "going against the grain" to employ a solution.

A meaningful organization is created through a consistent reference to core symbols and continuous symbolic activity that reinforce key values and beliefs (Deal and Peterson, 1994). These

---

FIGURE 3.3. EIGHT-STEP PROBLEM-ANALYSIS AND PROBLEM-SOLVING MODEL (REYNOLDS AND SILVER, 1987) EXHIBIT CONCEPTUAL FLEXIBILITY THROUGHOUT THE PROCESS (* EMPLOY INFORMATION SEARCH)

I. Understand the Problem (Problem Finding)
    a. Visioning—see the discrepancy between what is
       and what ought to be
    b. Be perceptive and sensitive
    c. Reframe/reform the problem

II. Identify Likely Causes*
     a. Look beyond the obvious
     b. Apply theory
     c. Look at self
     d. Draw on Experience

III. Search for Relevant Information*
     a. Verify hunches (know an informant's frame
        of reference)
     b. Seek sources of relevant information
     c. Set realistic boundaries (time factor)

IV. Set Specific Goals
    a. Establish clear objectives
    b. Avoid fear of failure, rejection, vulnerability
    c. Authority to make it happen

V. Identify Alternative Solutions*
    a. Optimize the solution rather than trying to
       satisfy everyone
    b. Expand one's mind beyond "the tried and the true"
    c. Imagine other solutions
    d. Seek ideas from other people

VI. Select Preferred Alternative
    a. Weigh pros and cons
    b. Understand the direct consequences and the
       short-range consequences
    c. Understand constraints
    d. Learn the indirect consequences and the
       long-range consequences
    e. Maximize vision/goals
    f. Consider ethical points

VII. Implement Preferred Alternative (Action Plan)
     a. Delegate
     b. Coordinate

VIII. Evaluate

FIGURE 3.4. THE SCHMUCK AND SCHMUCK (1983, PP. 60–61) SEVEN-STEP PROBLEM-ANALYSIS MODEL

I. Specifiy the Problem
    a. Situation—where you are
    b. Target—where you want to be

II. Analyze the Problem
    a. Limiting forces
    b. Positive forces

III. Generate Multiple Solutions
    a. Reduce the limit of forces
    b. Use"experts," such as people who have
       worked through similar problems

IV. Design Plans for Action
    a. Obtain input from implementers
    b. Conduct a reality check of "doability"

V. Forecast Consequences of Intended Actions

VI. Take Action

VII. Evaluate

FIGURE 3.5. THE NPBEA (THOMSON, 1993) SEVEN-STEP PROBLEM-ANALYSIS MODEL

Identify Input Elements of the Problem Situation

I. Analyze relevant information

II. Frame problems

III. Identify possible causes

IV. Seek additional needed information

V. Frame and reframe possible solutions

VI. Exhibit conceptual flexibility

VII. Assist others to form opinions about problems and issues take form as ceremonies, symbolic roles, metaphors, and stories. Leaders emerge through such activities because, often unconsciously, they want to experience and communicate deeper purposes and forge stronger human bonds among everyone in the school. School administration is shaped and fostered by a culture, a historically woven tapestry of values, beliefs, and symbols that supports an ethos of always striving to do better. Deal and Peterson state that high-performing organizations can have both parts of the paradox: quality and meaning, values and goals, artist and engineer, symbolic behavior and technical activity. In harmonizing these polarities, the ying and the yang, a principal will call on his or her spiritual and reality frames from experience.

Campbell-Evans (1991) explored the concept of framing. She interviewed a group of Canadian principals using situational simulations requiring decision-making skills. This process identified seven social values, seven political values, five basic human values, and three moral values affecting their decisions. These options added credence to the need for principals to reframe, reformulate, and consider situations and circumstances from different reference points.

Campbell-Evans maintained that decision makers and problem solvers are forced to make decisions within the contexts of their environments. Principals, therefore, analyze problems and make decisions in accordance with their own values, the values of the organization in which they operate, and the facts of each situation. The facts, however, are generally perceived first through the perceptual screen of social and political values present in the organization and second through basic human values. Social and political values include such things as justice, peace, due process, tolerance, cooperation, loyalty, trust, solidarity. Basic human values include such things as survival, happiness, companionship, self-respect, respect from others, and a sense of meaning.

IDENTIFICATION OF LIKELY CAUSES

In identifying likely causes in a problem situation, a problem analyzer might first look to self. How often do administrators spend time and energy looking for causes when they need only to look in the mirror? Consider the "bad breath" analogy. If you can't keep people in a conversation because you are wiping them out with unpleasant breath, then communication cannot take place. In this situation you are a blockage and, therefore, a cause. After addressing the self concerns, next look at the obvious and then beyond the obvious for causes. Causes are frequently determined by documentation of similar circumstances, by the application of theory, and by information obtained from reliable personal sources.

SEARCH FOR RELEVANT INFORMATION

Information search is the most critical part of problem analysis and problem solving. The "rule of thumb" is to take as much time as needed to get it right, but to move expeditiously in information-search work. If the administrator can build a solid information base, there is less likelihood that a decision will turn sour. Information search underlies all other parts of problem analysis. The principal must have a good sense of the organizational culture and of the expectations of participants, which include all stakeholders, or must be able to call upon a team member who does. The principal needs to know the sources of information, how reliable they are, and be able to verify hunches about the situation. Some extraordinary principals act on hunches because they know the situation and the players so well that they can project how a situation is likely to play out. An example is the strategic placement of an administrator at an assembly program to deter problems before they occur.

SETTING SPECIFIC GOALS (SEE FIGURE 3.3, P. 84)

During the information search or after it is completed, establish goals or targets for addressing the gap between the current condition and the preferred state. Limit the number of goals and make them simple so that all the "players" understand the expectations. *Only set goals that are reasonable and attainable and that you have control over.* Bluffs and speculations are dangerous moves and should be avoided. Have the authority and ability to make it happen. *Few goals and many methods* is a workable approach.

- ♦ Establish clear objectives that really address the problems, are definitive enough to address the discrepancy, and bridge the gaps between current conditions and the preferred alternative.
- ♦ Avoid fear of failure, rejection, and vulnerability.

Fear of failure relates to such things as power, position, self-esteem, risk taking, image, and so on. Also consider, as suggested in Chapter 1, the beliefs, attitudes, and values of the problem solver and of those who accept and implement the decisions.

Analyze the following vignette as a launching point for discussion concerning goal setting and fear of failure.

> ♦ A relatively new principal is considering a program that will greatly benefit a certain population of the students. However, in starting to obtain the program, the principal detected resistance from certain board members and certain central administrators. *In setting the goals for obtaining the program, what considerations need to be made in light of fear of failure, rejection, and vulnerability.*
>
> > • Another goal-setting question is, "Do I have the authority to make it happen?" Analyze the expectations, responsibilities, and position power needed to make sure that you have the authority or license to carry out actions.

Campbell-Evans' (1991) research identified six primary influences on principals' decision-making: three internal influences and three external. The three external influences were time, money, and factual information. The internal influences were concern for students, effect of decisions, and commitment of and to others to the decision. The high priority placed on the sociopolitical values in Campbell-Evans' study suggests that decisions and problem analysis were meeting the expectations of the larger system. Leithwood and Steinbach (1995) provide a detailed discussion of values and problem sharing. Values are the foundation upon which problem analysis rests and from which it builds.

IDENTIFICATION OF ALTERNATIVE SOLUTIONS

In this step, pull out all the stops. Brainstorm and list as many possible solutions as feasible to the situation. Consider resources and time needed. What are the emotional investments of the principal and others? What problems are the solutions likely to create? How comprehensive is the solution? What are short-term and long-term concerns? What is the possible public reaction? Involve others. One plausible alternative, even if it is rejected later is, "Don't do anything!" In some situations this worthy alternative should be appropriately applied. Think about someone you admire as a leader and imagine how that person might solve the problem.

♦ Optimize rather than satisfy everyone. This suggests an alternative or alternatives that have different success values for different audiences. Make the best choices rather than just talking about each expectation. (Figure 4.2, p. 117, in Chapter 4, provides added ideas for accomplishing this step.)

♦ The expansion beyond tried and true could mean that creative visioning is appropriate. Address the long-range possibilities.

♦ Imagine other solutions.

♦ Seek advice and counsel.

These concepts are frequently avoided by people who are self-serving, self-centered, selfish, unsure, insecure, power hungry, and so on. Research, current literature, and history tell us that when many minds come to grips with a problem situation, the result can be numerous alternative solutions rather than singular thought or direction. Information can be power and the more valid input there is, the more powerful can be the outcome.

SELECTION OF PREFERRED ALTERNATIVE

In selecting an alternative, even if it is to do nothing, there needs to be a plan for accountability for the action. Often, a good plan is to select an alternative that lets other people help you. But overinvolvement may hinder progress ("too many cooks spoil the broth"). The selected alternative should address each goal. The alternative also must meet the test of such factors as impact, direct and indirect consequences, long-range consequences, constraints, and ethical considerations.

In selecting a solution weigh the consequences, including ethical considerations. For each alternative, apply the questions taken from the model (Figure 3.3, p. 84). Does the solution address the vision? Does it address the discrepancy? Is it "doable"? Who are the winners? Are there any losers? What are the problems of the solution? In each stage, the principal should be open-minded and employ conceptual flexibility.

Upon completion of the many processes involved in problem analysis, the principal now seems ready to solve the problem. This is true to a point. Problem solving means making a decision and then following through with action. However, implementation should include an action plan that will address the causes, vision, goals, and objectives established by the individual responsible for the decision. If problem solving goes awry at this point, then the process lacks credibility and so will the decision maker.

IMPLEMENTATION OF PREFERRED ALTERNATIVE (ACTION PLAN)

In implementing the alternative selected, make sure that the players have the needed information and know the ramifications of the solution. Assure that procedures, expectations, and workable conditions are in place to help move events toward success. Who are the players? What needs to be in place to ensure success? What application has the best chance of success? How will one know if it has been successful?

EVALUATION

The evaluation is based on whether or not the goals were reached and the ideal state/vision was accomplished. Results of people-problem situations are likely not to be just quantitative. Consider the qualitative elements and recognize the tradeoffs involved. The evaluation must be clearly stated and address the discrepancy between the "is" and the "ought." Evaluation questions include: Has the discrepancy been addressed? What specific measures will determine success? Was the vision reached? What is the next step?

This brief problem-solving model outlines some steps to guide actions. The steps could be learned and practiced by principals in all problem-analysis situations. The other models mentioned in the text (Figures 3.4 and 3.5, p. 85) describe steps similar to the Reynolds/Silver model, but each expresses key steps in slightly different terms.

CONCEPTUAL FLEXIBILITY AND COMPLEMENTARY ASSOCIATIONS

If they are to be influenced by open-mindedness, sensitivity, and awareness, then principals must understand the concept of flexibility. If we know that we operate from fairly set and defined frames of reference, as has been suggested, then in reframing the problem situation, the problem analysis process will demonstrate conceptual flexibility (Reynolds and Silver, 1987). Conceptualists have opinions about most things and they do not have to think long about an issue to have opinions. Conceptualists seldom consider the fact that others may have different opinions (Maurer, 1991, p. 232). In problem analysis and in decision making, a leader may encounter a situation with a perception gained from another person's frame of reference. For example, if the principal has information from a source that in the principal's frame of reference is valid and reliable, the principal's perception of the information is that it is true. This information may conflict with information that a teacher is in a position to share with the principal. Add to the mix that the person who gave the principal the information is an arch rival, and there is the possibility that the information could be tainted. The principal must be careful, especially if an information search has shown that there may be a conflict in the making. This potential conflict creates a condition where the principal should review the frame of reference to derive second opinions and good analysis upon which to build subsequent decisions. This scenario requires the principal to exhibit conceptual flexibility, that is, open-mindedness, sensitivity, and awareness. The principal must not overreact to the situation or to a person, but should conceptualize the "big picture" and its attending problems. Perhaps a leadership team or an ad hoc group will help with the decision process. Complementary association supports collegiality and allows others opportunities for creativity and leadership in forming reasoned opinions and strategies.

Problems abound, but problem finders do not. Why? Some people are not trained to identify problems; others do not try; others do not recognize a problem as an opportunity. Some people need help in seeing beyond the obvious or the routine (Achilles and Norris, 1987–1988). Air force squadrons have wingmen and assistant and associate positions are created. In work with the Johari Window, Luft (1969) indicated that many of us cannot see the obvious without feedback or through *complementary associations* made popular through expressions such as, "You watch out for me and I'll watch out for you," and "You scratch my back and I'll scratch yours."

Complementary associations can be critical to a principal's success. A complementary association is the pairing or teaming of people who possess skills that when added to the group's total potential provide a synergistic effect, which can be applied to problem analysis. Frequently, people who step into administrative positions will surround themselves with people who think, act, and react the same way that they do in an effort to have reinforcement and support, and perhaps to achieve a certain comfort factor. Administrators should examine the idea that a better way of establishing a team is to seek out complementary associations based first on identifying the tools, abilities, and traits needed to be a successful administrator. A second step is to analyze those job requirements in which you are less inclined to show interest. Seek people as colleagues who have strengths in these identified areas. This develops a synergism that builds strength for navigating the shoals of administration. Complementary association is an administrative team concept that requires considerable thought in assembling the team. The caboose is not always at the end of the train. It suggests flexibility; that is, when trains reverse, the caboose becomes the front.

Although the principal may be the locomotive, the principal works with others to mold an organization that responds effectively to its problems. The principal helps create a safe and orderly environment that assures clients that problems will be identified and solved in a timely, appropriate, and open manner. Leaders have been replaced because they could not anticipate problems and had insulated themselves from the day-to-day tumults. For example, when a principal is visible in the building and tries to be where the action is likely to be, there is less likelihood of adverse behavior. This means being in halls, lunchrooms, and other gathering spots around the school, as well as at extracurricular activities. Seek to create an expectation that problem analysis is one path to improved operation of the school.

CONCLUSION

This chapter on the Problem of the Solution has moved from problem finding to problem solving through a series of activities, theories, and models that suggest means by which people can address problem analysis. In problem solving, the steps to decisions may impact all stakeholders within the organization. Perversely, the solving of problems leads to the realization that problem analysis/problem solving in all likelihood will uncover more problems (problems caused by the problem of the solution).

The problem of the solution suggests such terms as discovery, data gathering and sorting, experimentation, creativity, sensitivity, understanding, perception, action, change. Sprinkled into this recipe are mythology and just plain luck. The time, energy, and interactions involved in this important work help to explain that the principal is always busy and that a principal's work life is full of excitement.

Chapter 3 dealt with the processes of problem solving. Chapter 4 offers opportunities for expanding problem-analysis skills. In Chapter 4, problem analysis (problem finding and problem solving) is moved a step or two further by the suggestion that decisions have consequences. For discussion, we place problem-solving decisions into three categories:

♦ Decisions for change, going against resistance.

♦ Decisions to flee the responsibility of making a decision; a do-nothing solution.

♦ Decisions to adhere to whatever thought is prevalent at the time.

The following case studies provide opportunities to practice problem analysis processes, with particular attention to problem solving. In working through the cases, try using the steps of the problem-solving model presented in Figure 3.3 (p. 84). Also consider carefully the roles of information search and of complementary associations.

CASE STUDY: HOW FAR DOES THE SCHOOL GO?

The Community. The town of Reese had a population of nearly 80,000 and was located in the Bible Belt section of the Southeast. Religious beliefs were very evident in this town as were many negative feelings toward minorities, especially African Americans.

The School. Davis High School was located in the town of Reese in the central part of South Carolina. The school was the eighth largest school in South Carolina and was highly regarded in the state as an education leader. The school had been selected as one of the top 10 model schools in the United States approximately 5 years ago. The principal, Don Smith, was very popular in Reese, and was highly respected throughout the state. Davis

High School was composed of 55% white and 45% black or other minorities. Racial problems had never been evident at Davis, partially because of staff and faculty interaction with students and parents, and also because of excellent programs, especially athletic teams. The community took a tremendous amount of pride in Davis High and the students there. This was evident in very strong parental involvement in all programs at Davis.

The school year was into November and things at Davis were operating smoothly with only normal problems occurring. On a Monday morning two white parents appeared at Mr. Smith's office very upset. They told Mr. Smith their names and he immediately recognized them as parents of two 10th-grade girls. The parents told Mr. Davis that black male students had been calling their homes asking to speak to their daughters. The parents did not think too much about this situation until one of the parents saw her daughter get into a car with one of the black males at the mall over the weekend. This incident started both parents investigating into the situation further and they found out that the girls had been dating these guys for a month. The parents said they also knew that their daughters were walking around school with these guys. The parents wanted some advice from Mr. Smith on what to do. After talking with the parents longer, Mr. Smith indicated that he would check into the situation and get back to them.

On Wednesday morning of the same week, a parent of a ninth-grade white male came to see Mr. Smith. He told Mr. Smith that his son was running around with a group of white guys that called themselves the "Gray Boys." These guys wore their hair very short on the sides and combed straight up on top. They also wore black-hooded long jackets with professional team logos on them and baseball caps, also black, turned sideways. They listened to rap music and idolized black entertainers and sports figures. The "Gray Boys" did not attempt to hide their feelings that they wished they were black and preferred to be seen with blacks as opposed to whites. They attempted to date black girls only. The parent expressed concerns about his son's situation to Mr. Smith and asked for advice. Mr. Smith told him he would look into the situation and get back with him.

Later that same day, four fights broke out at school involving white boys and the "Gray Boys." The white boys took exception to the style of dress of the "Gray Boys" and made some derogatory comments that led to the fights. On Thursday morning a fight broke out between a black male and two "Gray Boys" because one of the "Gray Boys" had called the black guy's girlfriend the night before. As a result of these fights, many rumors traveled around Davis High that there would be more serious fights and that some students would bring weapons to school for protection.

On Friday, two "Gray Boys" were caught with a pistol at school. They were arrested and expelled. When this news spread, frightened students called home and told their parents and requested permission to leave school. Over 200 students left school early; Mr. Smith was bombarded with questions and concerns the remainder of the day. The radio, television, and newspapers picked up the story and reporters bombarded the school to get information.

The Challenge. Place yourself in Mr. Smith's position. Can you identify three key problems? How would you handle this situation as presented? Use sound problem-finding processes to help you identify one or two key problems. Work through one or more solutions using one or more of the models in Figures 3.3, 3.4, and 3.5 (pp. 84–85).

CASE STUDY: STUDENT DISCIPLINE

Jeremy, a seventh-grade male student at Meigs Middle School, pulled on the back of Jenny's bra and then let it go. Jenny ranted, fussed, and fumed, and this got the attention of Ms. Kelly, the classroom teacher who was on hall duty between periods. Upon hearing the commotion, Ms. Kelly entered her classroom. By this time, Jeremy was teasing Jenny. Things became heated and got out of hand. Jeremy shoved desks out of the way and began to chase Jenny around the room.

Ms. Kelly knew Jeremy's history of temper tantrums and told him to go into the hall to cool off. This was also a means of getting him away from Jenny. Being told to leave the room upset Jeremy even more. When he got to the hall, he punched the glass casing that enclosed the fire extinguisher, cutting the knuckles and fingers on his right hand. Ms. Kelly heard the glass breaking and ran into the hall to see what had happened. She sent Jeremy to the office to have his hand looked after. Ms. Kelly had no choice but to write a discipline referral for destruction of school property.

The next day, Ms. Kelly overheard Jeremy bragging to his friends and to the coaches about punching the glass casing and not getting into trouble. Ms. Kelly spoke to Mrs. Nelson, the principal, about the referral. Mrs. Nelson said that Jeremy would be punished, but she did not know when she would get to it. The following week, Ms. Kelly approached Mrs. Nelson again about Jeremy's referral. Ms. Kelly explained that Jeremy had been boasting about not being punished because he and the principal were good buddies.

Mrs. Nelson said that Jeremy did have a temper, that his temper landed him in trouble last year, but that was no excuse for his behavior. She told Ms. Kelly that she and Jeremy had long discussions last year about his temper and that he had promised to work on controlling it. She reassured Ms. Kelly that Jeremy would be punished, but that she hadn't had the time to do it yet. Mrs. Nelson explained that she had spoken to Mrs. Meyers, Jeremy's mother, when she came to school to pick Jeremy up the day of the incident. Mrs. Meyers told Mrs. Nelson that she felt that Jeremy should be punished for his behavior. *What response would you have to Mrs. Meyers? As principal where would you go for your information search? What issues are involved in this situation and what might be problems of the solution? What might be the reactions from both sets of parents to the events between and involving both students? Divide your work into the three categories below.*

Action Steps	Issues	Problems of the Solution
1	1	1
2	2	2
etc.	etc.	etc.

CASE STUDY: OVERSIGHT OR NEGLIGENCE?

Happy Valley School is a very close-knit community of teachers and students. Not very much goes on within the school or the community that everyone does not know about. The principal and most staff members grew up in Happy Valley and have come back to work there. Several teachers were former students of the principal. Mr. Williams had taught at Happy Valley for 7 years before becoming principal, and he has been principal for 22 years. He is very conservative, deeply religious, and his philosophy is, "if it ain't broke, don't fix it."

Although Mr. Williams maintains a neat, clean school campus, several teachers have complained about the tennis courts, which had fallen into disrepair. The nets were gone and only the steel poles remained. The lower elementary teachers used the area for organized play; the upper grades used it for kickball.

The physical education teacher used it when the grassy area was too wet for play activities. Several students had collided with the poles while playing, but no one had been seriously injured. At faculty meetings the teachers suggested that the poles should be removed and the holes filled in to reduce the danger to running children. The project was suggested for PTA endorsement. Each time an injury occurred because of the poles, teachers complained, but Mr. Williams did nothing.

One day Ms. Bailey took her first grade class outdoors at her assigned time, and because the grass was wet from heavy dew she decided to play "on the courts." While the children were involved in a game of tag, Susan Jones ran into the steel pole causing serious injury to her upper lip and front teeth. The rescue squad was called and Susan was rushed to the hospital. She required several stitches and, in time, plastic surgery. Within 24 hours of the accident the poles at Happy Valley were removed from the tennis courts.

Susan's father visited the school the very next morning and wanted to know why the poles had not previously been removed. One of the nurses who helped Susan told Mr. Jones about the teachers' complaints. It got to the point that Susan's dad physically pushed Mr. Williams and vowed to see him in court.

♦ Reorder these questions into the proper sequence.
  • Where does awareness come into this situation?
  • What are the legal implications and where would you find this information?
  • What are the likely causes that need to be addressed?
  • What is the ideal state in this situation?
  • What are some alternative solutions?
  • What is the best solution from your perspective?
  • How would you evaluate the solution?
  • What goals might be set in this situation?

♦ Consider...
  • Why hadn't OSHA inspections forced the removal of the poles?
  • Does this need to be part of the "given" in the scenario?

- ◆ What is the role of each of these…
  - Information Search?
  - Complementary Associations?
  - Frames of Reference?
  - Reframing?
  - New Information?
  - Testing of Solutions?

CONCLUDING THOUGHTS

The initial chapters focused on the idea that problem analysis is a combination of problem finding and problem solving. There has been particular attention to identifying a problem carefully, and to suggesting structure and steps to guide the principal to a good solution to a well-framed problem. If both the problem-finding and the problem-solving steps are accomplished, the principal is well along the problem-analysis path. Vignettes and cases interspersed with the narrative provide opportunities for reflection, for discussions, and for practice in applying the ideas presented in the text. But there is more.

The principal cannot do everything alone. The better equipped that others in the school are for dealing with problem analysis, the more likely that problems at school will be routinely handled well. Solutions to one set of problems may lead to added problems, and problems that are opportunities for growth will offer possibilities for leadership and change. Influencing problem sharing and leadership is also the possibility that some problems may take on lives of their own. Some problems are not easily contained or solved.

In the next sections, we consider the relationships among problems, leadership, and change. Some fairly detailed cases offer grist for testing problem-analysis skills and for applying some of the concepts and models presented in Chapters 1 through 3. Figure 1.5 (p. 8) in Chapter 1 shows some of the steps in problem analysis that move the effort into a leadership and change mode. After the problem of the problem and the problem of the solution, there are two steps that extend problem analysis to the entire school community: problem sharing and leadership in decisions.

4

PROBLEM SHARING, LEADERSHIP IN DECISIONS, AND CHANGE

Conceptual flexibility suggests that the analysis of problems is much like predicting the path of a tornado. Environmental conditions play a great part in structure and process of problem analysis. Meteorology, earth science, astronomy, human behavior, pure chance, and even chaos all seem to have an influence in predicting a tornado's path. Commercial fishermen know that if they steer right or left away from a storm, the water spouts might cover them no matter which way they move, but that if they keep steady on course heading in the direction of the spouts, the spouts generally change direction and leave the boat alone. Storms in any form, including difficult problems, sometimes take on lives of their own and seem to have personalities that parallel human behavioral characteristics.

In Chapter 2 (Figures 2.4 and 2.5, pp. 44–45) we categorized problems as academic and structured or messy, real life, and practical. Until now we have treated problems as if they were quite rational, and that a rational approach to problems would benefit the problem analyzer. This is true much of the time. Generally the better you perform in problem-analysis, the better the base for your decisions and your subsequent actions. Yet, some problems just get out of hand. We call those problems *runaway* and *rogue* (R+R) problems. It seems that no matter what you do with one of these problems, it's bound to be a lose-lose situation. You need, then, to search for a *win* out of the mess.

- ◆ A parent objects to the assigned novel for the freshman English class. Neither the district nor school has a written policy on this issue. The angry parent threatens legal action. *Why does this have R+R potential? What problem-analysis steps are in order?*

Successful problem analyzers are students of human and of organizational behaviors. These serve as foundations for understanding how persons function in these environments. Besides just the cognitive or rational approach to a problem, the problem analyzer also calls on affect or feeling, including factors such as intuition, whimsy, luck, serendipity, sensitivity, tacitness, and hunches. Although the principal is in charge of problems at the school site, part of the principal's task in staff development is to bring along all faculty and staff to be part of the problem-analysis team. If this is done, then in the language of the sailor in the introduction, the principal needs to chart a new course and steer a straight line to the next situation, which is problem sharing.

♦ A handicapped teacher is consistently late to class and the other teachers begin to complain to the principal. *How should a principal use the concepts of open-mindedness and sensitivity in this situation?*

PROBLEM SHARING

One type of problem sharing was discussed under the heading of complementary associations, a form of participatory management. Bailey (1991) explained that in group problem analysis and subsequent decision making, the leader should take into consideration the talents of all members of a group. A leader allows group members to use their combined skills in the problem-finding process. In each situation, group leadership may change in accordance with the skills of the person who has unique knowledge of the solution. In these proceedings, the leader becomes a facilitator who takes on the responsibility of drawing upon the skills and creativity of others. Bailey also stated that in a planning process, it is necessary to get all persons tuned in to the problem. Brainstorming is particularly effective in group planning and thinking activities.

♦ The school board has just passed a policy that forbids teachers from retaining elementary pupils in grade. The community will not stand for "social promotion." *Engage in information search. Plan to brainstorm possible solutions with stakeholders. Whom will you invite to this session? Who will be in charge? Will the same people be in charge at all stages? Rank-order the brainstormed solutions based upon various "Frames" (Chapter 2, Figure 2.6, p. 47). How will you communicate with the public the research on the negative effects of grade retention?*

Bredeson (1993) examined teachers' and principals' perceptions and how organizational change affected their relationships. He found that cooperation, understanding, and trust among faculty members, including the principal, built an enabling environment for creativity in problem analysis and decision making. This positive change in relationships and creativity is a first sign that faculty members are exhibiting conceptual flexibility and collaboration in collectively forming reasoned opinions.

Sharing decisions using complementary association can be a highly effective way to implement educational change. Faculties who embrace collaborative decisions and make new strategies to replace the "older" ways engage in complementary association. This can be a form of problem analysis, but before any groupwork can be effective, the individuals need to be ready to work on a team. This preparation will require leadership and team-building by the principal.

The beliefs, attitudes, values, and frames of reference that a team eventually uses can be better understood if individuals come to problem analysis and to decision-making situations with a strong understanding of self. When people understand the values that drive their own actions, they can better come to grips with their own decision-making and analysis styles as well as those of others. If a principal is to share problems and the problem-analysis process successfully, the principal should have both a keen sense of knowing people and some framework for guiding the choices of whom to rely upon.

♦ A young woman who is sent to the office for a verbal altercation with another student becomes even more upset upon encountering questions from the principal. She bursts out of the office and down the hall shouting "F--- you!, F--- this school!, and F---

everybody!" *How can beliefs, attitudes, and values impact on a principal's process in addressing this problem?*

Each person embraces situations from a primary perspective. The Myers-Briggs Type Inventory (MBTI) results help a person identify the "type" the person resembles in particular situations. These MBTI "types" are described by terms such as sensing, thinking, introvert, extrovert, and so on. The types are polarized: extrovert/introvert, sensor/intuitive, thinker/feeler, and judger/perceiver. Most people show characteristics in both fields of each type; however, one type very often dominates reactions, thinking processes, and communication. *Extrovert* types are fast to act. They dislike complicated procedures and are impatient with long, slow jobs. They like to have people around and they communicate freely. *Introvert* types like quiet for concentration and they tend to be careful with details. They may have trouble remembering names and faces. They enjoy extended work on one project without interruption. They work contentedly alone and may be reluctant to communicate.

Sensing types dislike new problems unless there are standard ways of solving them. (Consider Getzels' presented problem, Chapter 2, Figure 2.3 (p. 43).) They enjoy using skills already learned more than learning new ones. They usually reach conclusions step-by-step and are patient with routine details. *Intuitive* types like to solve new problems and dislike doing the same thing over and over. They enjoy learning a new skill more than practicing it and work in bursts of energy powered by enthusiasm, with slack periods in between. They put "two and two" together quickly and are impatient with routine details. Intuitives are, however, patient with complicated situations and follow their inspiration, good or bad. They often get their facts a bit wrong but are very loyal. People who are intuitive in their behavior often cause people around them to remark, "How did he do that?" "How did she know that?" Generally, people who rely on intuition have a great deal of self-confidence and are in charge of situations without the badge of office. Consider the value of this type in brainstorming for new ideas and in analyzing problem situations to identify problems (Getzels' discovered problem, Chapter 2, Figure 2.3 (p. 43)).

Thinking types are relatively unemotional and unaware of other people's feelings. They may hurt someone's feelings by proceeding without regard for others. They like analysis and order and can operate without harmony. They tend to relate best to other thinking types. *Feeling* types are aware of other people's feelings and enjoy pleasing people, even in unimportant things. They need occasional praise and dislike telling people unpleasant things. They relate well to others and tend to be sympathetic, if not empathic.

Judging types function best when they can plan their work and follow the plan. But, they may decide things too quickly and frequently may not notice new things that need to be done. They tend to be satisfied when they have reached a judgment or closure. *Perceiving* types adapt to changing situations but may display some reluctance for making decisions. They may start many projects and have difficulty in finishing them. They tend to be curious and welcome new slants or insights.

> ◆ A new assistant superintendent gathers his 12 high school principals and 8 program directors for their first meeting of the year. He doesn't make introductions, although many new people are in the crowd. He proceeds with his agenda, controlling most of the meeting. Little time is allotted for discussion of items. He fires off questions, but often doesn't permit people to respond adequately. Some people begin making hooded eye contact; others stare straight ahead with no apparent engagement with Mr. Assistant Superintendent. At the end of the three-hour meeting, the new administrator smiles broadly and says, "Thanks, guys, for a great first meeting." *How would understanding personality "types" help all members of this meeting? What problems might occur down the road for this aspiring superintendent and his communication methods? What sensitivity issues need attention?*

Understanding these "types" is useful in considering problem analysis, including information search, and problem sharing. In previous chapters, we described how the principal had opportunities for personal growth, leadership, and for expanding the possibilities of a good problem solution by using problem-sharing steps. The increased involvement and diversity, however, also bring challenges that demand a broader frame of reference to problems than just finding a quick fix.

Political, sociological, and anthropological frames all affect a person's process of problem analysis. Savery and Souter (1992) found that to understand a frame of reference for decision making in schools, one must consider such factors as policy, discipline, economics, teaching load, parental involvement, and time allocation. These factors form a frame of reference that can help a principal see a variance in individual responses, but the principal must remember that these factors form the structure for other people involved in problem analysis. For example, if a principal and faculty members are in a situation where the decision-making process involves powerful people who could have a negative impact on their jobs should the decision go against the powerful people, the various individuals' frames of reference could be security, survival, and so on. Since each decision is influenced by a person's personal skills, experiences, and frame of reference, the chances get greater and greater that someone on the problem-analysis team will represent the diverse frames of reference in the larger community, if the principal involves several members of the faculty in the problem. Problem sharing may help the principal to anticipate new problems and expand the decision options.

In interviews with principals, Ashbaugh and Kasten (1987) determined that the factors that impacted the most difficult decisions they made were *personalities,* including family values, religion, political heat, experience, traits, physiological and psychological make-up, and so on; *organizational concerns* such as expectations, tradition, culture, hierarchy, and time; and *transcendent values* such as personal welfare, long-range plans and goals, and personal health. People added to the problem-analysis team will likely expand the personalities, organizational concerns, and transcendent values and options, and both expand the decision options and assure that diverse points of view are at least considered, if not incorporated into solutions.

Millerborg and Hyle (1991) studied legal and ethical considerations used by school administrators. In clearly defined situations, principals made clear, ethical, and legal decisions. In less clearly defined situations in a legal sense, those that often occur in schools, the principals tended to turn toward ethics rather than toward law. Secondary principals relied on ethical procedures as opposed to legal decisions more frequently than did their counterparts in the lower grades. Although the legal issues may be fairly clear, ethics pose their own problems when the principal shares the problem-analysis process.

People might more readily agree on legal issues than on normative "should" issues. What implications do subjective ethical questions have for problem framing, especially when law is taught in administrator training programs more frequently than ethics? Where do principals attain or obtain their knowledge of ethics? Are ethics inherent in peoples' frames of reference such as beliefs, attitudes, values, and experiences? The larger the problem-analysis team, the more likely conflicting values and ethics may surface. The differences in responses to these questions between the secondary and elementary administrator may reflect experiences. Sheer weight of opportunities to participate in problem-analysis/problem-solving and decision-making in secondary schools may be a factor. Age, experience, and degree of child versus content focus might also differentiate between elementary and secondary principals' approach to problems—plus, the degree of parental involvement.

LEADERSHIP IN DECISIONS

Decision making is the standard by which a principal will ultimately be judged. In its assessment criteria the NASSP uses the terms "decisiveness," "decision-making," and "judgment." Although assessment centers do not judge decision quality under decisiveness, they do look for it in other categories, notably judgment. Yet many principals are proud of their decisiveness, the act of making decisions. At first they may not emphasize whether the decisions are good or not. Their focus is on being decisive. In administrator training programs, there is a wide discussion of situational practice which seems to be one wave of the future for principals. As a part of problem analysis, we emphasize quality and appropriateness of the decision. A good decision is based on clear and correct problem finding and cogent and careful problem solving. By using case studies and vignettes, administrators can "practice without punishment" the processes of problem analysis, and they can then discuss the decisions.

 ♦ A teacher reports to you that the custodians are spending large amounts of time in the janitor's storage room laughing, smoking, and talking. The building and grounds are deteriorating to the point that teachers are lucky even to have their trash cans emptied at the end of the day. Carpeted areas are rarely vacuumed; tabletops and desks are dirty and dusty. Noncarpeted floor areas are seldom mopped. Custodians each have been given areas to be responsible for, but no schedule of duties is mapped out for them and no follow-up is made by any supervisor. The teacher is annoyed that for the second day running there are no paper towels in the teacher's rest room and she wonders if it has ever been cleaned.

Custodians have been socializing with the students who, as punishment for violating school rules, have been assigned work detail under the supervision of a custodian. They have even been seen buying the students soda and potato chips from the machines in the teachers' lounge.

The teacher has two main concerns. She is outraged by the sloppy work and also feels that the students in the school are getting a bad example from this situation. *Consider the potential for problem sharing and for leadership in decisions. Whom should the principal involve? What information search should precede any serious action? Generate a scenario for problem analysis in this vignette.*

Problem Analysis   =   Problem Finding
↓
Problem Solving
↓
Decision Making

(➜ *= leading to*)

INTERNSHIPS AND PRACTICE AS PROBLEM-ANALYSIS SHARING

Research and current literature strongly suggest that the more clinical experiences an administrative candidate can receive, the better equipped the candidate might be for an administrative position. Clinical experiences in problem analysis built into internships allow candidates to work through actual situations to learn problem-analysis skills, to develop conceptual flexibility, and to explore problem sharing. Milstein, Bobroff, and Restine (1991) commented that administrator internships not only allow students an opportunity to apply knowledge from coursework, they also let them determine if they possess the ability and desire to be administrators. Since much of a professional's work is to help resolve "people problems," preparation programs should emphasize both problem-analysis skills and experiences in problem sharing as a step toward problem resolution with lasting benefits. The National Policy Board for Educational Administration (NPBEA, 1989) suggested that university preparation programs ought to develop long-term formal relationships with school districts as a way to provide meaningful clinical study, field residency, and applied research. The NPBEA recommended that practitioners who serve as supervisors of these internships hold status as clinical or adjunct professors. Such partnerships have the potential of reducing practitioner concerns that administrator preparation programs rely too much on unstructured or artificial experiences and problems.

It is shortsighted at best to think of internships or praticums only as a small piece of administrative training. The too typical one-semester-long internship is usually limited to one or two hours per day and usually comes out of the hide of the trainee during planning period, lunch, and before or after school. Money and time are not readily available for full-time release, so clinical experience must be supplemented with case studies built upon day-to-day administrative practice related to problem analysis, staff development, and change. Often by sharing problems with other administrators, principals learn to defuse petty, but potentially peevish, situations that arise in school settings. Practice via case studies helps them build problem-sharing skills.

◆ A new elementary principal has inadvertently created a rift between herself and the assistant superintendent. The relationship between the two administrators is almost at a standoff. Whenever a request is made from the school for much needed materials, supplies, or maintenance, the request is denied. The assistant superintendent has been in her position for many years and is a very strong personality to deal with, especially when it comes to money, as she is in charge of all district finances among other things. To add to the new principal's woes, the assistant superintendent's spouse is the bookkeeper/secretary at the elementary school. The first-year superintendent's position in this is "hands-off." *Apply a problem solving model to this case. (Figures 3.3–3.5, pp. 84–85). Especially consider conceptual flexibility and problem sharing.*

Some problem analysis goes well beyond the school's borders, but the situation has serious repercussions for the school. Involvement of others, including persons from other agencies, is not unusual. Agency collaboration is often a valuable resource in problem solving.

◆ **Case Study:** Substance Issue Has Substance

On Friday at 7:45 A.M. a student told the principal that he was caught with a substance (marijuana) at State University (SU) over the weekend. He said that the principal would probably be hearing from SU as he and two others were charged by SU officials with possession of a controlled substance. The two other people were underage, but this young man is legally an adult. He also explained that he spent the night in the local jail. The young man stated that he was sorry for what he had done, as he was not "into drugs." The principal was impressed with the young man's forthrightness and told him that since this event occurred out of the school's jurisdiction, and so on, if the student complied with SU's initial sanctions, the principal would do nothing more at this time. The principal advised the young man to steer away from further involvement with any controlled substance.

Later that same day the principal discovered three young people in a bathroom that was off-limits during class time except by permission. The principal noted a strong odor of marijuana and that the young men, too, had a strong scent of the drug. The principal realized that one was the same student who confided in him earlier that morning concerning the drug incident at SU. The principal asked all three to walk toward his office. He walked behind them to his office located some distance (150 to 250 yards) from the rest rooms. As they were walking toward the office, the bell rang for classes and students flooded the hallways. The principal watched the young men as closely as possible under the circumstances. When the principal arrived at the office, the assistant principals each took one young man into separate rooms for surveillance. The principal took the young man who was involved at SU into his office.

The principal had instructed the assistant principals to ask if they could search the students' book bags and clothing. He suggested that the assistant principals smell hands and clothing for the scent of marijuana. The superficial search of clothing and book bags turned up no marijuana; however, each administrator separately noted a strong odor of marijuana smoke on the clothing and hands of all three students. Two students indicated that the third student did provide them with some "weed," that he had had in his possession, and that they were all smoking in the rest room. The student alleged to have provided the drug was the one involved at SU. The two students who made the accusations were then asked to write exactly what transpired, and to date and sign the statements. Each administrator also signed as witness. Meanwhile, the student alleged to have supplied the drug denied his involvement and claimed that he just "walked in" on the others as they were in the act.

Other factors also came into play. The students were skipping a class and were at opposite ends of the school from where their classes were located. The rest rooms were off-limits during class except by special permission, which they did not have. The student accused of supplying the drug had a beeper, which by state law and school board policy was illegal. With this information in hand, with the information received from the student about the situation over the weekend, and with his denial of any involvement, the principal was required by law to inform the local police about the probability of a narcotics violation on school grounds. The principal asked a secretary to call the students' parents.

A local detective arrived soon after being called. The policeman informed all students of their rights and then interviewed the two younger students about the statements they had made that the older student possessed the drug. They reiterated their story and thought that the third student still had the drug. This gave probable cause, so the police officer entered the office where the student suspect was located. In the company of the principal, the police officer asked the suspected student if he minded being subjected to a strip search. The student said that he would allow the search. A search was carried out and no drugs were found.

The young man's father arrived on the scene. The principal and the detective filled him in on information to date. The father was obviously upset and distraught. The young man was asked if he minded taking a drug test. Both he and his father indicated that this would be unfair since the young man had already admitted to using marijuana on the weekend and that it takes days for the drug to leave the bloodstream. The principal, assistant principals, and the police officer said that the test would also tell them about recent use of the drug. The father and the young man agreed to the test. They left the principal's office at about 2:30 P.M., Friday. The young man was tested at about 4:00 P.M. the same day.

On Monday morning, both parents of the young man tested for drug use spoke to the principal in his office. They were angry with the principal and supported their son who they maintained was innocent. They also claimed that the other two young men had called over the weekend and recanted their stories. The principal reviewed the evidence with the parents and said that he would schedule a meeting with them as soon as the test results were returned. In the interim, the parent of one of the other two students withdrew his child from school and sent him away. The father of the third young man told the principal that he was sending his son to another state to live with his aunt who had the means and the environment to take care of him. This father disclosed that his son's mother had died and that under the circumstances he felt unable to handle the young man and his current behavior.

Late Monday afternoon, while in conference with another family, the principal was asked to talk to the parents of the young man who was involved in the drug test. The principal stepped out of his conference and was handed a copy of the test results. All tests were negative! The principal noted the "smugness" on the face of the parents. He told them that he was in conference at that time and that he would contact them by noon the next day to set up an appointment. The superintendent had been informed on Friday about the situation and was given an update on Monday.

On Tuesday morning, the principal became deeply engrossed in another drug situation that consumed the whole day. However, he did call the young man's parents and asked them to come in the next morning when they would determine the disposition of the case. During the day (Tuesday), the principal had an opportunity to talk to other people concerning the drug test case, local police officers (one who was involved in the strip search and a juvenile officer), the superintendent of schools, a school attorney, a university professor, and two assistant principals. Each person offered advice and counsel to the principal, but more importantly, each showed support and confidence in whatever decision the principal made.

Consider this case from the view of a person who has been categorized by MBTI as a *senser/judger* and from the view of another person categorized as an *intuitive/perceiver*. *Senser/judgers* might demonstrate these traits as characteristics or tendencies:

- They like rules, regulations, and proper procedures.
- They call upon learned, tried and true skills and processes.
- They are usually very methodical in actions and planning, and patient with routines.
- They are good at precise, factual work.
- They will develop a plan and then follow the plan.
- They strive to "wrap things up," that is, to bring closure in a neat package.
- They often make lists of things to do or of new ideas.
- They have a tendency to make snap decisions and judgments; they are hard to interrupt and generally not flexible.
- They tend not to see what effect they have on other people.
- In making decisions and judgments, they tend not to change.

Intuitive/perceivers might demonstrate some of these qualities or tendencies:

- They are usually bored with routine tasks, duties, or responsibilities.
- They enjoy a challenge, but when initial excitement abates they move on.
- They demonstrate "right brain" tendencies, but also apply logic and deductive reasoning.
- They often will act without definitive direction or reason.
- They thrive on "tough" situations.
- They always seem in control of the situation.
- Often they are not precise.

♦ They demonstrate flexibility and can deal with ambiguity.

♦ They will put things off and work in spurts.

♦ They have rapid ideas and often don't take time to write them down or prepare lists.

How would a sensor/judger address the following questions? How would an intuitive/perceiver respond? Would the two types produce similar solutions in each situation?

♦ List five alternatives a principal might have in this case. Prioritize the five.

♦ What other information is needed and how can it be attained?

♦ How is each element listed here an important consideration in this case?

Due Process	Reliability	Problem Sharing
Miranda Decision	Consequences	Leadership
Evidence and Search	Time	Liability
Probable Cause	Alternatives	Decision and Purpose

Consider some ways that problem sharing and involving others in leadership for change through problem analysis can expand a principal's options and increase the possibility that various frames of references come into play. Allison and Allison (1993) discussed the "telescope effect" in problem analysis, or studying a problem through both ends of a telescope. Both attention to detail and taking a broad view of a problem were associated with judged quality of response. Persons judged as having handled the problem-solving task better than others tended to view the problem in both ways. It was as if they stepped back and took a broad, inclusive view of the problem and its context by looking through the wrong end of the telescope. They also looked closely at specific elements by looking through the magnifying end. They viewed the possibilities microscopically and globally; they didn't exclude possibilities.

The inclusive view involves problem sharing, conceptual flexibility, sensitivity, and awareness. If time allows, the leader should use both the telescopic and the panoramic view in problem analysis and in decision-making. Yet, by problem sharing and by including others, a dynamic interaction is possible where each individual can have both a panoramic and a telescopic view in the problem analysis; people collectively, as the group, can also have both views; and there can be discussion of all viewpoints relative both to problem identification/clarification and to problem solving. This interaction will expand the alternatives and improve the problem-analysis outcome. This situation is depicted in Figure 4.1.

FIGURE 4.1. THE VALUE OF PROBLEM SHARING IN ACTIVATING "BOTH ENDS OF A TELESCOPE" PROCESS (ALLISON AND ALLISON, 1993)

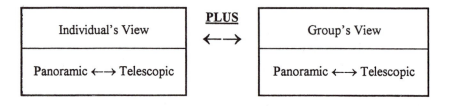

The potential for this type of productive sharing is available in nonroutine problems that allow enough time for interaction as part of the principal's personal growth, the information-search process, and the professional growth of faculty through shared experience in problem analysis. The potential is there, but the principal's leadership is needed to make it happen. A second benefit beyond problem analysis is also possible.

By expanding the problem-analysis team and thereby getting broad representation of values, political views, frames, and so on, there are increasing opportunities to involve those people who are affected by the solution and by implementing the decision. Involvement at the problem-defining and problem-solving levels increases the potential for acceptance of the decision. Implementing a decision is initiating change. Problem analysis and decision making are conceptually linked; good decisions, enhanced by clear problem analysis and problem sharing, lead to positive changes.

Consistent, effective decision making enhances a principal's success. Part of the process is established or demonstrated through the principal's experience, which includes the gaining of expertise by repetition, or by doing the same or similar things well over and over (Routine Problems). Another factor is intuition. Some principals demonstrate an uncanny sense about problem situations. These are effective pieces to problem analysis and decision application, but they alone are often not sufficient. Gorton (1987) offers two theoretical constructs to suggest that a successful problem solver also needs a decision-making process to use as a guide or model. The literature and research provide considerable information that supports both theoretical constructs in the Gorton argument.

+ A rational or normative approach to problem analysis suggests a format or process based on a logical sequence of steps such as those suggested in Chapter 3, Figures 3.3, 3.4, and 3.5 (pp. 84–85). A model of this type implies that the problem analyzer has considerable control in the process.

+ Gorton's second theory suggests that culture, climate, situations, and circumstances really control problem analysis. Problem solvers have little actual control and at best have limited influence over their environments; consequently, there is little use for the systematic analysis as put forth by advocates of the rational or normative camp. Problem analysis and decisions are influenced by personality, values, beliefs, attitudes, frames of reference, previous experience, and even intuition, more than by reason or intellect. Until now, this text has emphasized the normative or rational approach to problem analysis. There is, however, room for diverse views.

ROGUE AND RUNAWAY (R+R) PROBLEMS

Gorton's second theory includes what we have called Rogue and Runaway (R+R) problems. These problems may be so political or grounded so deeply in beliefs and values that virtually no amount of data, logic, or rational consideration will seem to influence anyone involved in the problem. The atmosphere surrounding the problem is contentious and confrontational (perhaps even litigious), with little apparent possibility of consensus or of reaching common ground. These problems take on lives of their own, often swelling out of proportion much like mob action when a few people can instigate a stampede. Sometimes in R+R problems, the best—and most important—first option is to gain some moderate control of the mob. Rational problem solving can't occur until the runaway rogues are at least minimally restrained. Rogue problems probably still can be handled by careful problem analysis and rational work as well as by any other way, if they can be handled at all. These problems take extra skill, often requiring the principal to involve persons who can help to diffuse the pressures, such as facilitators trained in group process or in consensus building.

One strategy is to form teams of community persons to work on the problem. This will broaden the administrator's base of operations and reduce the possibility that the problem is being fueled and fanned by only a few people making a lot of noise and showing up over and over again. The team will have an advisory role in suggesting solutions while listening to diverse opinions, but the members of the team get to have their own say, too. This approach is based on the ideas that a few genuinely disgruntled people can generate a great deal of willful opposition to demonstrate power and control, and that most people who are satisfied with the status quo or who seek peaceful change generally don't initiate confrontations. This larger group may stay uninvolved until a crisis stage is reached unless the principal reaches out to seek the help of this large group.

Teams of community persons get many people to listen, to consider alternatives, and to help verify which data support the problem and provide directions to a useful decision. In this case, the principal shares the problem, increases information search potential, and helps assure that a vocal minority does not impose its will at the expense of the majority. Similarly, a good problem analyst will also avoid what Alexis de Tocqueville called "the tyranny of the majority," wherein survey results or vote counting can obscure good points made by minority groups to the extent that preferred solutions are lost. Consensus building offers the opportunity for all groups to have input, to receive some consideration of their points of view, and for finding a decision that diverse groups can buy into. Yankelovich (1991) provides 10 steps to achieving what he calls common ground or resolution (Figure 4.2). These 10 steps offer a path to follow when confronted with R+R problems.

FIGURE 4.2. TEN STEPS TO RESOLUTION AND TO FINDING COMMON GROUND (YANKELOVICH, 1991, PP. 160–179)

Ten Rules or Guides for Finding Common Ground
and Resolution

1. Assume public and experts are out of phase.

2. Do not depend on the experts to present the issues.

3. Learn the public's preoccupation and address it before discussing any other facet of the issue.

4. Give the public the incentive of knowing that someone is listening and cares.

5. Limit the number of issues to which people must attend at any one time to two or three at most.

6. "Working through" is best accomplished when people have choices to consider.

7. Leaders must take the initiative in highlighting the value components of choices.

8. Move beyond the "say 'yes' to everything" form of procrastination.

9. When two conflicting values are both important to the public, seek resolution by tinkering to preserve some element of each.

10. Allow sufficient time.

R+R problems, like wild horses, will kick off in directions that the principal really is not able to control. This occurs when a problem that might have been handled at the building level is escalated into central office or some other level, or when a problem becomes a political football. In these situations, a principal is deprived of taking problem-analysis steps at an appropriate time—the problem just runs away. Typically, in R+R problem situations people get territorial or defensive, or they may act without thinking it through simply adding to the confusion. In dealing with R+R problems, at least try to determine the source person, and if this person really is beyond reach via reason and discussion, try to discover if the source person listens or responds positively to anyone else. If so, those few persons might assist in getting through to the source of the problem.

In the following case study, put yourself in Pat's role. Work through the case twice. First, try to figure out the cause(s) and source(s) of the problem. Consider the role of time, circumstances, and decisions made by persons other than Pat. Write a scenario for the actions you would take. Then go back and analyze the problem using the steps in Figure 3.3 (p. 84). Compare your two results.

♦ Case Study: *Who Is in Charge Here?* A Rogue and Runaway (R+R) Problem. *In examining this case, use the background information provided.*

The year was just wrapping up and the teachers had checked out. Pat sat in the office contemplating the achievements of the past few years, particularly those from last year. The accomplishments seemed substantial. All in all, Pat believed that the year had gone well. Next year's senior class would represent the fulfillment of the many goals that had been set and met since that group had been ninth graders when Pat became principal.

Taking over the principalship of Overlook High School had been a bit of a surprise, but the process was not unusual for this school district. Three years ago, a few parents had complained to Central Office (C.O.) about vague "things" at the school, and C.O. had acted promptly to install a new principal, Pat. No one from C.O. had discussed with Pat any particular problems or complaints about the previous administration. Pat had a reputation for school successes and had been an effective leader, but so had the previous principal.

This year had been quite good. The teachers were progressing nicely in their transition from being "just" classroom teachers to becoming highly skilled professional educators who looked beyond the classroom and school to understand what was actually occurring in American and international education. Several teachers were sought after as presenters at state, regional, and national meetings to share their ideas, the school's progress on a school-to-work activity, the faculty's efforts at problem-based learning to make classes more exciting, and things like that. Faculty development was, perhaps, Pat's greatest achievement and strength.

One thing was bothersome. One teacher had commented that last Sunday at one of the community churches, someone was circulating a petition about the high school. There was little more to know other than it was just another rumor, but this had surprisingly similar tones to the removal of the prior principal. At that time, a petition and unrest had developed just after the teachers had left for the summer, so that the principal was alone; there was no easy way to get teachers back or to convince the PTA to consider the issues. The comment about a petition simply reinforced a couple of rumors and Pat made a note to check into it later.

One other thing lingered. Throughout the year, Pat had felt unsupported and beleaguered by a C.O. superior. Pat questioned decisions and wanted to know why certain conditions had to be, especially when there was little or no research to support them. Even common sense suggested that some of the C.O. mandates wouldn't help student achievement. This slight professional disagreement had seemed to escalate throughout the year, right from the first conversation that Pat and Chris, the C.O. administrator, had at the beginning of the year when, with no provocation, Chris said that Pat was the only principal that questioned things. Strange language indeed. At this point, Chris was a newly appointed C.O. administrator, had not been to Pat's school, had not had any direct personal or professional experiences with Pat, and had only made these comments based on Pat's participation at C.O. meetings.

One of the assistant principals broke into Pat's thoughts to report that she had heard more about the rumor and had evidence that a few people were circulating a petition about "events" at the school. Pat and the assistant principal decided that it was time to call C.O. and ask Chris for some assistance. They called, and in a couple of days called again, but the C.O. administrator was never available to work with them on this problem. The two of them decided to put things on the back burner until after graduation.

Chris attended graduation, and said that this was the best high school graduation in the district. However, just before Pat went on stage to hand out diplomas, Chris off-handedly referred to a recent meeting at the C.O. with a group of disgruntled parents from the community of Pat's high school. The C.O. Administrator said that Pat had not been called to the meeting so the group could openly discuss the concerns. This comment unsettled Pat, but graduation proceeded well.

At the office later that day, there was a note that Chris had scheduled Pat's evaluation conference in four days. This was a surprise as there had been no mention of this evaluation before, and Pat and Chris had not discussed any formal objectives for this year, as objectives were not required every year in the district evaluation plan. With a sense of foreboding, Pat began to assemble information for the evaluation. Pat still had no idea what the community group was concerned about and, therefore, could not prepare any discussion or rebuttal if this should be a topic at the evaluation conference. Pat did decide that concerns of the group should not be an issue at the evaluation, as there had not yet been any opportunity to investigate the concerns or to meet with the people. If there were problems, why had the group not come to the PTA? In fact, it was unusual that someone would make a petition rather than come to the school to discuss concerns. Strange. Soliciting signatures on a petition seemed more like a witch hunt than an attempt to deal with substantive issues. Still, Chris had not yet provided any information to Pat about this event, or about the group meeting.

While preparing for the evaluation conference, several people called to tell Pat what they had heard, bits and pieces of the rumor mill. When each piece of information became available, Pat reviewed it in the limited context. In each case, there was no such issue that Pat knew about. Pat decided that rumors, rather than concerns based on fact, must be circulating. One rumor was that Chris had been contacting other people to get information, but still had not contacted Pat; worse, the rumor was that Chris had been seeking advice from other professionals in the district and even had contacted the next-year PTA president to learn if she knew about these so-called concerns.

This rumor was verified when Pat made a few calls. Pat also learned that a meeting was held at C.O. with a seven-member group claiming to represent many people. The group provided a list of demands from "Parents Actively Involved Now" (PAIN) at the high school. Although the PTA had active committees to deal with issues, no one who complained at C.O. had used the PTA committees. Indeed, many of the C.O. meeting attendees were parents of students at the middle school. Their children would not come to the high school until next fall.

Several days after the meeting at C.O., Chris and Pat met for the evaluation conference. Pat finally obtained a list of the problems and allegations. The list was handed to Pat by Chris' secretary as Pat left the evaluation conference. Still no discussion had occurred. Only one or two items on the entire list had any substance, as far as Pat knew. The plans were for Pat and Chris to meet with PAIN at the high school. Pat could respond to concerns then, but not in a rebuttal tone. Pat had 10 workdays to prepare comments regarding each concern on the list. Some seemed easy to explain, as they related to substantive and quantitative data: student achievement scores, won-lost records in sports, the number of athletic teams, Pat's presence at extracurricular events, and so on. Given the clear lack of facts to support the group's claims, Pat began to consider what would be appropriate evidence of school progress and goals.

Pat invited the high school administrative team to attend the meeting, knowing that Chris would bring C.O. people and that Chris would run the meeting for awhile. On Tuesday, the second workday of the 10 that Pat had counted on, Chris' secretary called to say that the meeting was rescheduled for Wednesday at 9 A.M. Pat was furious. Chris had unilaterally rescheduled the meeting a week and a half earlier.

The day of the meeting found Pat and two other members of the administrative team facing a six-member community group and C.O. people, including Chris and the district athletic director, who was a bit of a surprise, since Pat had heard that parents were mostly concerned about academics and the school climate.

Chris ran the meeting, acceding to each demand as it was presented and even promising that the group could be an unofficial advisory committee to Pat and the teachers, all without consulting Pat. Pat pointed out that the PTA had committees that dealt with school issues and that these parents would be welcome to join, but Chris cut this discussion off, indicating that this group would be a special committee to watch after things. Chris also promised to visit the school in the summer, meet with teachers to check on "climate" and Pat's leadership, and work with Pat to get things up to a certain standard—one as yet not told to Pat.

When Pat began a discussion of obvious errors of fact on the group's claim sheet, Chris cut Pat short, indicating that time was running out and that the meeting was over. Pat was left holding a sheet of group "demands," and copies of factual materials compiled for the meeting but that nobody had looked at and nobody had discussed. Chris told Pat to keep the district athletic director, Chris' designated appointee for this case, informed of events at the school. Pat sat in the office and wondered, "What's next? Am I answering now to the athletic director?"

Pat reviewed the progress at the school, looked at notes from the meeting, and decided that it was pretty much a no-win situation, given the lack of C.O. support and the fact that Chris had taken over. Chris had made decisions about how Pat would work, not what needed to be done. This seemed to infringe on professional relationships beyond repair.

(1) What is the problem(s)? (2) What you would have done at various times, (a) when you first heard about the "rumor," (b) when you first heard about the C.O. meeting, (c) at the meeting in Pat's (your) office. (3) What might have been appropriate action on the part of (a) the supervisor (Chris), (b) Pat, (c) any other players in this drama? (4) How would a Case Record have been helpful? (See Appendix A.) Work through this case using the Case Record form after the fact. Discuss output with colleagues. What other data would you like to see in considering this?

Review material presented in "The Rest of the Story" below and return to questions 1–4 above. *How would you change any of your responses to the questions—if you would change any? If Pat decides to leave the principalship, would you support that decision? Why or why not?*

♦ "The Rest of the Story"

OVERLOOK H.S. Principal's Office
OVERSIGHT School District

June 3, XXXX   (Document prepared but not discussed at meeting with "PAIN")

What We've Done... *Facts About Progress at Overlook H.S. (930 pupils)*

The administration and staff of Overlook High School always welcome parent and community involvement. Because providing progressive educational services is such a huge undertaking, school personnel especially solicit the constructive assistance of parents in educating their children. We invite and encourage interested school supporters to become involved through the school's PTSA. Many ad hoc committees now exist to work collectively on all aspects of the school's program. Parties interested in collaborating may contact Pat Smith, the principal, at ABC-1234 or Marilyn Brown, PTSA president, at ABC-4321. Meetings for the committees have already begun. Many wonderful goals have already been met, and we would enjoy having more people working with us. The following considerations may be helpful.

• Test scores have remained relatively stable for the past 15 years, despite the sharply changed demographics of this large attendance area.

• Incoming 9th graders scored considerably below expected achievement in math and language arts on 8th grade standardized tests; often from 25% to 40% below.

• Approximately 25% of Overlook students attend 4-year colleges; the rest attend technical schools, enlist in military service, or enter the job market.

• The top 25% of our students average about 1000 on the SAT; the top 10%, about 1025. Three years ago the average SAT score was under 900.

- The number of students not eligible for a State diploma because of failing the Competency Exam averages in the single-digits, from senior classes of over 130.

- Dropouts have dramatically decreased in the past 3 years (from 54 to 17 presently).

- The academic, vocational, and fine arts programs have expanded in all areas. About 30 new courses or levels have been added in the past 3 years to meet the needs and interests of students. Because Overlook is a relatively small school, this accomplishment is difficult, given the necessary distribution of teaching responsibilities. assignments, and available resources.

- Advanced Placement (AP) courses are difficult to offer—but necessary to the total school program—for a variety of reasons. AP and honors courses require additional preparation, usually extensive reading followed by complex writing assignments and tests. Teachers offer special study groups for AP courses, but students are often unwilling to attend for several reasons: after-school work/activity schedules, personal motivation issues, frustration, etc. Despite these obstacles, efforts to build this program are paying off. Most AP courses are increasing in enrollment, especially in math, and students benefit from exposure to advanced studies. Teachers have already begun planning for study group sessions for next year.

- Future plans include offering college credit courses directly on Overlook's campus through the services of Oversight Technical College Transfer Program.

- Government in Action began 3 years ago with six students; we now have more than 30 who write legislative bills, research government functions, practice public speaking, and attend a mock State legislative session in Capital City. Next year, Overlook has a candidate for Government in Action Governor.

- Our faculty members have written about $75,000 in funded grants in the past 3 years, attended dozens of local, state, and national conferences, and have presented successful Overlook programs at several conferences.

- An Overlook student was Oversight's Interstudent Council President, the representative officer of all 15 student council presidents.

- Community and civic service are now incorporated in Beta Club, National Honor Society, Junior Civitans, and Interact clubs. Activities include tutoring, charity and volunteer services, and community and church work.

- The graduating class of 135 earned approximately $350,000 in scholarships. This amount does not include financial aid or grants, and represents a $150,000 increase in 2 years.

- Overlook students have recently won top state awards in marketing, entrepreneurship, and journalism. Two business students competed nationally, and other students won state writing competitions.

- Two students this summer were selected for national leadership training in Washington, DC, as well as being mentioned in *Who's Who Among High School Students.*

- Two Overlook teachers were selected as part of a national group of 100 math and science teachers for training in math and science integration using technology.

- Overlook piloted the "Senior Practicum" for the school district this past year. We combined traditional research with product formation and presentation to make research and writing more relevant in the School-to-Work program.

- Several English teachers belong to the State University writing project cadre and write for personal publication.
- SAT preparation and Core Skills Test remediation classes were added last year.
- Approximately 35% of the student body participate in some type of athletic program, up about 5% in 1 year.
- Twelve coaches have been hired in the past 3 years; none was hired during the preceding 5 years.
- Approximately 25% of the student body earn some level of honor roll distinction.
- The business department has doubled in size in the past 2 years and now hosts many more academically advanced students in computer and accounting courses. Industrial technology has doubled its enrollment in 2 years and has many more college-bound prospective engineers and architects as students.
- Tenth graders will be eligible for a new program next year at the Regional Career Center that will introduce them to technical and professional careers in manufacturing and engineering. This new endeavor is a result of direct input from Overlook's administration and faculty.
- Foreign language classes have also doubled; we are anticipating offering a third language in the near future with an additional exploratory program in Japanese.
- The staff developed a premier career planning brochure, used as a model throughout the state.
- Science classes have a new instructional format: more laboratory activities, new technology (computers, CBL calculators), problem-based learning, etc. Honors-level classes have dramatically increased in biology and chemistry.

OVERLOOK H.S.
OVERSIGHT School District

June 6, XXXX

P. Jones, Ed.D.
Superintendent
The Oversight School District
P.O. Box XYZ
Oversight, DT

Dear Dr. Jones:

For over 11 years I have been an administrator in The Oversight School District. I have enjoyed my principalships in middle and high schools and have extended my formal education to earn a doctorate in educational leadership. From these experiences, many other exciting opportunities have developed that reflect the quality of my professional work and which enrich the total schooling effort I represent. My training has enabled me to motivate and lead my staffs to higher levels of professional competencies in staff development, curriculum, instruction, and leadership. As stronger advocates for student success, Overlook teachers have advanced their competencies as highlighted speakers at state and national conferences. With remarkable dedication and aptitude for grant writing, in the past 3 years, they have received approximately $75,000 of national and state grant awards.

Additionally, my beliefs about life-long education, the transition between levels of schooling, support for at-risk students, and the need for school, family, and community collaboration have expanded the role of the traditional teacher to that of professional educator, one who has the knowledge base and resources to understand the influence of multiple risk factors on student success. To address the needs of all students, my practices include a wide array of student support services in order that teaching and learning remain education's priorities. Training and program implementation in conflict resolution, higher-order thinking skills, school-within-a-school, and problem-based learning are among the philosophies and skills that I have advanced in my work.

Results of these beliefs and activities have included several publications, including a book about full-service programs, plus book chapters, and professional papers. Presently I am coauthoring a second book. My participation in local and national professional organizations permits me to share new ideas with my coworkers.

Please consider me as an open candidate for positions becoming available at the district administrative level. My interests are wide, and I believe that my abilities and experiences include most major areas of our field, including curriculum, alternative education, human resources, staff development, grant writing, career education, and student services at elementary, middle, and high school levels.

Thank you for the opportunity to express my desire for new professional responsibilities. I believe that my administrative successes and experiences could now be used to the benefit of other programs and people. Enclosed is my résumé for your review.

Pat Smith

Pat Smith, Ed.D., Principal

Enclosure: Résumé

"Who Is In Charge Here?" is an example of R+R problems that take on lives of their own. They are fueled and fanned by actions seemingly outside the administrator's control, but clearly the administrator must take some action or the problems continue to worsen.

R+R problems offer challenges to the problem analyst; they may involve personal feelings, values, politics, attitudes, and beliefs. They may involve personal attacks where rumor and innuendo escalate issues and concerns, perhaps when parents are frightened or don't know what to do, or where demographic changes in a community are met by teachers and community members by, "This isn't the way it used to be," rather than by problem analysis and action. A penchant for the nostalgia of the "good old days" (that probably never were) causes people to propose remedies for R+R problems that may or may not have worked in the past. The solutions to past problems without modification and adjustment for today's contexts probably won't suffice as solutions for today's different problems. Yet experience in problem solving will help even in these situations. The use of a problem-analyzing model will offer the principal a surer path to success than simple guesswork.

The discussion of the problem-solving model in Chapter 3 (Reynolds and Silver, 1987), included the idea that the problem solver could be a major contributor to the problem and a factor in the solution. Recall Pogo's, "we have met the enemy and it is us" dictum. Review Appendix A and note that one category of the Case Record is "Possible Causes: Self Based." The principal should consider what she or he contributes to the problem. Sometimes doing the right thing at the wrong, or unacceptable, time presents a problem if the school community hasn't accepted that it may have problems. "Kill the messenger," is one possible outcome in this situation. Sometimes you're dammed if you do, and dammed if you don't.

IMPLEMENTING DECISIONS FOR CHANGE

The first, and perhaps the most important, step in implementing a decision is to secure its acceptance on the part of those who will be most affected by it. One way to gain acceptance is to involve the people in the process as early as practical. One procedure for doing this was discussed earlier as problem sharing. Whether a decision maker can gain acceptance of a decision depends on many factors, including the perceived inclusiveness and openness of the process, the decision maker's prior successes, and the perceived legitimacy of the administrator's position within the organization; that is, does the decision maker have the power and influence to effect the decision?

After attending to the antecedent conditions of good problem analysis, the principal (and other stakeholders in the problem) will be ready to implement the problem solution(s). This act of implementing represents a decision to change some condition that caused or aggravated the problem situation at the outset. Change and communication processes and theories become important tools now. In gaining acceptance for the decision, the principal might ask :

- ◆ Does the decision solve the problem?
- ◆ How many stakeholders were involved in the process?
- ◆ Does the decision demonstrate a sensitivity for the organizational culture?
- ◆ Were the ethics of the situation addressed appropriately?
- ◆ Did all persons involved understand the decision and the resulting action plan?
- ◆ Was follow-up established to evaluate decisions and actions?

If those involved in the decision can answer "yes" to these questions and find that the process used by the principal is reasonable and correct, they may be comfortable in the legitimacy of the decision maker whether they agree with the decision or not. Frestas (1991) stated that decisions based on perception, insight, experience, and ethical integrity are generally well accepted by stakeholders and go a long way to establishing legitimacy for the principal's future decisions.

As surely as the solving of one problem will lead to one or more new opportunities to practice problem analysis, the implementation of that one problem's solution is likely to be the culprit in generating new challenges to the principal's leadership. Rather than leaving the implementation of a decision to chance, the successful principal continues the rational process of problem analysis by developing and using an action plan to guide the change process generated by a new decision. The efficacy of change will be related to the clarity, cogency, and comprehensibility of communications surrounding the problem, the decision(s), the proposed solution(s), and the chosen implementation processes. A logical way to plan for the change and to track its implementation is to design an action plan as a matrix that addresses key elements of communication on one axis and the levels or steps in a change process on the other axis; to implement a decision is to communicate and to change. The major elements of communication are shown here:

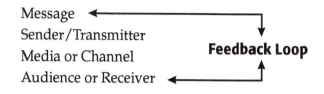

Message
Sender/Transmitter
Media or Channel   **Feedback Loop**
Audience or Receiver

Authors and researchers have described steps, levels, or processes leading to the implementation of some innovation. Taken together, these levels can be considered as stages of the change process. Although various authors use slightly different names or terms for the stages, content analysis of how these authors use the terms suggests that there are four fairly similar and identifiable stages or levels. The first three levels (I–III) are shown here to demonstrate the similar idea but different terminologies expressed by the authors.

Authors (cited in Figure 4.3)	I	II	III
Rogers	Awareness/ Interest	Trial/ Evaluation	Use/Adoption
Berman & McLaughlin	Initiation	Implementation	Incorporation and Institutionalization
Achilles	Dissemination	Demonstration	Diffusion
Yankelovich	Consciousness Raising	Working Through	Resolution

Descriptors from the authors listed in the note to Figure 4.3 are grouped into four levels (I–IV) as shown in Figure 4.3. Level IV is a self-renewal or collegial stage that comes just after institutionalization of the decision, and that helps structure monitoring and continuous improvement.

In the four change levels shown in Figure 4.3, five elements of communication and a statement of how each level relates to change are developed into a matrix. The matrix is designed to

FIGURE 4.3. A COMMUNICATION/CHANGE MODEL

COMMUNICATION ELEMENT: message, media, channel or sender, audience(s).	CHANGE PROCESS LEVELS and DESCRIPTIONS			
	I - Initiation	II - Implementation	III - Incorporation	IV - Institutionalization
Relation to Change	Awareness/Interest; Dissemination of Information; Consciousness Raising.	Trial/Evaluation; Demonstration; Working Through.	Use/Adoption; Diffusion; Resolution.	Constant Renewal of all Persons in the Process.
Message (Purpose)	Understanding. Conceptual Control.	Skill Building. Expanded Knowledge Base.	Transfer of Skill and Knowledge.	Refinement of Skills and Knowledge. Relationships.
Method(s) and/or Media: Sender or Transmitter	Journal; Memos; Conference Presentations; Mass and One-way Communication.	Demonstration; Group Work & Discussion; PBL; Case Study; Question and Answer (Q&A); Two-way Communication.	Simulation; Role Play; Practice with Feedback; Q&A; Training; Use of an Action Plan.	Reflection; Self-monitoring; Synthesis/Application; Peer Coaching and Discussion.
Targeted Audiences	Individual; Large Groups. Undefined/Uncertain	Individual; Small Groups; Job-Alike Groups. General Definition.	Individual; One-on-One. Specific Persons.	Precise and Specific. Individual.
Assessment Strategies.	Paper and Pencil; Oral Comments; Memory; Cognitive.	Observation; Discussion. Practice Cognitive/Affective	Observation of Use; Critique: Self Reports. Conative	Individual Long-term Growth. All Modes.

A communication/change model to guide leadership actions in implementing decisions for change. The model suggests how the change may be initiated and monitored. Terms are combined from several authors: E.g., Rogers, 1962; Rogers and Shoemaker, 1971; Hughes and Achilles, 1971; Achilles and Norman, 1974; Berman and McLaughlin, 1974 and 1978; Yankelovich, 1991.

help guide leadership actions in implementing decisions for change. Descriptions within the matrix provide guidelines to help the principal plan and monitor the decision and changes that occur based on the completed problem analysis. This model actualizes the "Leadership in Decisions" dimension presented in Chapter 1, Figure 1.5 (p. 8), "Organizing Concepts and Ideas Related to Problem Analysis." Terms are combined from several authors, including Rogers (1962), Rogers and Shoemaker (1971), Hughes and Achilles (1971), Achilles and Norman (1974), Berman and McLaughlin (1974, 1978), and Yankelovich (1991). This particular model is demonstrated in Achilles (1988, pp. 48–49).

Each problem situation that culminates in a decision to change is an authentic assessment of the principal's problem-analysis ability. Making a decision, however, does not end the problem analysis. The action that comes after the problem analysis is the real observable outcome. The savvy principal will be as careful to follow a process or model in implementing the decision as she or he was thorough in using a problem-analysis model to guide the problem-analysis process.

ACTIVITY

After the fact, select one change that occurred in your own district. Trace its history and track its success by using the ideas in Figure 4.3. Attend carefully to the use of communication processes and determine if attention was given to each stage, or at least stages I–III of the change process. Once you have traced a successful change in your own setting, return to the R+R problem, "Who is in Charge Here?" and see how many steps were omitted in that problem. What would you do to fill in each gap?

This chapter concludes the presentation of the key elements in problem analysis as presented in Chapter 1, Figure 1.5 (p. 8). Chapter 5 offers some cases to allow each reader to sharpen problem-analysis skills and to practice concepts presented in the text.

5

CASES

After a brief summary of the problem-analysis process, this last chapter offers case studies for role playing and for opportunities to practice without punishment the processes of problem analysis. For purposes of practicing case analysis we suggest that you follow the format developed in the Reynolds and Silver model presented in Chapter 3, Figure 3.3 (p. 84). Every step is not applicable in each case; however, the model will guide you through a systematic thinking and association process for problem analysis. Appendix B may help establish ways to address these cases.

We began this book with discussions of the importance of careful problem analysis and the creative effort that is behind good problem finding. Many professionals besides Getzels (1985), whose example was presented in Chapter 2, recognize the creative elements of problem analysis. Cornish (1995) described a book in which the author Min Basadur said that most people think of problem solving as a "drag," but that, on the other hand, people believe that creativity is fun and a mind-taxing intellectual activity. Basadur connected creativity and problems by saying that "creativity is in fact a problem solving exercise" (p. 49). Creativity is usually stimulated by some challenging problem. After the challenge is addressed, resulting in some innovative idea, the next step is implementation. Basadur's eight-step problem-solving model, which he called "Simplex," has three major stages: (1) finding problems, (2) developing creative solutions, and (3) implementation. Basadur's model begins with problem finding, which he liken edto being an inventor. His last step is taking action. The rubric that runs through this model is creativity.

To be a successful problem analyzer, the principal must be creative, perhaps as opposed to devious. A careful re-reading of the Getzels' (1985) excerpt presented in Chapter 2 will help to highlight the creativity needed, especially in analyzing "discovered problems." The questions might be, "How can we (I) be creative in finding and defining the problem in this situation?" and "How can we (I) solve this problem in a manner where all players benefit in some way?" This chapter contains principal-related management and leadership activities incorporated into a few case studies. These exercises require you to respond to real-life situations, to think reflectively and creatively, and to practice all elements of problem analysis.

Problem Analysis = Problem Finding + Problem Solving

↓

Decision Making

↓

Planned Implementation
Steps and Evaluation

(➔ = *leading to*)

INSTRUCTIONS FOR THE CASES

Read each case completely to obtain a sense of what the case is all about. Read the case again for content, characters, circumstance, and issues. Other readings may be necessary. After you feel comfortable with the characters, circumstances, and facts, analyze the case by first identifying the problem or problems and then by following a model or structured process, such as the Reynolds and Silver model (Chapter 3, Figure 3.3, p. 84). Plan to follow a model to provide a framework and a process to achieve a creative solution. Assume the role of "principal" and address as many of the cases as needed for you to become comfortable in using a structured problem-analysis process. For each case write a brief narrative to describe succinctly how you would proceed at each step of the model described in Figure 3.3. This narrative should include your problem statement (refer to Chapter 3). In analyzing these cases, consider such subjects as communication, current issues, interpersonal relations, race and gender relations, equity, stakeholder relations, organizational culture, organizational management, and curriculum. Some questions that you might ask for each step for each case are: What are the issues to be considered? What are the possible consequences of each decision? Will the decision have a chance to fuel a rogue and runaway (R+R) problem?

REFLECTIVE THINKING

Appendix A contains a comprehensive discussion of the value of reflective thinking in problem analysis. Review Appendix A. Consider the use of reflective thinking and the requirement of time for reflection at key steps of problem analysis, such as during information search. Duplicate copies of the Case Record worksheet to use in your work on the case studies.

Kirschman (1996), Kowalski (1995), and Daresh and Playko (1995) all advocated case study use and reflective thinking as steps to improve administrative decision making. Kirschman suggested that the case study method is a low-risk learning technique and that case studies are especially useful in the development of skills such as analysis, critical thinking, information search, and reflective thinking. We have adopted Schön's (1983) suggestion that reflective action is a form of artistry that is especially critical when circumstances are less than rational. In the real world of problems, and especially of rogue and runaway (R+R) problems, practice is not always predictable and the perversity of R+R problems may allow administrators to apply artistry (a quality developed by refining professional knowledge on the basis of experience) in problem analysis.

In an interview, researcher Lee Shulman stated, "I'd like to see much greater use of cases, much like what was done in law and business education" (Brandt, 1988, p. 3). The expanded use of problem-based learning in administrator preparation adds a dimension of simulation, similar to a case study approach, that fosters problem analysis. Through considerable practice, one may begin to tame and normalize the wild fluctuations that drive problem analysis into the corner where each problem is so unique as to require artistry. Over time, and with experience to level some of the pinnacles or to fill some of the pits, problem analysis can become routine, more like a craft and less like an art, where a craft is the artful but fairly predictable application of experience plus science to some product or process. Consider problem analysis as part art, science, and craft, refined and honed by reflective practice and experience.

CASES FOR PRACTICE IN PROBLEM ANALYSIS

The cases that follow demonstrate a range of problem-analysis options. In working through each case, first divide the case and its problem elements into the corresponding major category shown in Chapter 1, Figure 1.5 (p. 8). (Problem of the Problem, Problem of the Solution, Problem Sharing, and Leadership in Decisions). Next, consider the general ideas that cluster around the major category that you have chosen for each problem element. Apply some logical problem-analysis model to move you to a solution. Finally, consider how you would implement your decision and evaluate its impact..

Follow the steps in the model in Chapter 3, Figure 3.3 (p. 84). Clearly identify the problem(s) and write a problem statement. Discuss your problem statement with one or more colleagues. How does your problem statement stack up with the elements of a good problem statement? (Review the section on problem statements in Chapter 3.)

CASE 1: FIGHTING

Ricardo (Ric), a male Hispanic student, moves to your school. Immediately, he starts talking to other students about gangs and his involvement with them. Several days later another student tells the principal that Ric is pushing and shoving as if to start a fight and is talking about gangs. This student says that he is not going to allow more pushing. The principal calls Ric to the office and explains school expectations and the consequences of fighting on the school grounds. He gives the student advice for success and getting along at his new school.

Ric befriends several other white and Hispanic students during the next several days. Two weeks later, on Friday after school, there is a confrontation in the parking lot between these students and three black students. This confrontation is over a black female student and stems from remarks to the black student during the pep rally that took place at the end of the school day. A teacher on duty in the parking lot stops the oral confrontation and the groups leave school after exchanging some challenges.

A fight takes place over the weekend, off campus, between some blacks and the new group led Ric. On Monday before first lunch, some of the black students approach one Hispanic student wanting to know what he was doing telling others that one of their group had sold him (the Hispanic) some slack weed. The black student doing the talking threatens the Hispanic student with a beating. The shouting escalates. Ric then comes up and starts making derogatory remarks to the blacks. He drops his bookbag, begins to make gang hand signs to the blacks, and states that he would fight all of them. At this point, he swings and hits one black student, knocking him against another black student. A brawl begins. Students fight across the commons area. Ric is the only Hispanic in the fight. Several blacks are hitting and kicking him as the fight moves. Teachers and administrators hurry to break up the fracas. As they pull students apart, one student curses and swings at a guidance counselor, while trying to rejoin the fight. When the principal arrives, Ric is being held by a teacher and the other participants have been moved away from him. The principal directs students to calm down. He begins moving onlookers to classes or to lunch. Things begin to settle down, but while Ric is being held aside by a teacher, a black student who was not involved in the fight walks up and hits him in the head. Fighting erupts again. Teachers and administrators identify fighters and escort them to separate offices. Police are called according to school policy, and the fighters are arrested.

Six people are involved as key actors in the fracas: the Hispanic who was originally approached by the blacks, two blacks who were initially cursed and hit by ric, two other blacks who joined in the fighting, and Ric. One was the black student who hit Ric while he was being held by a teacher.

The six students involved subsequently admitted to their respective roles in the fight. Further investigation found that Ric is a member of a gang known as "Folk" and had been in gang trouble at his previous school. The Hispanic student involved in the initial confrontation moved out from the crowd to avoid being hit and was not in the fight. Likewise, the black student who did the initial talking never became involved in the brawl. This particular student was already under a probation contract with the Board of Education and if he committed another offense, he would have to appear before the Board for review.

In your opinion, what elements of this case are examples of good (or not-so-good) art, science, and craft? What are the far-ranging implications for this incident and for the development of new policy and procedures regarding student behavior at the school?

With whom would you share these problems and solutions? What future problem situations might you anticipate as a result of your "solution" to this problem? To explore this last question, list several alternative "solutions" and the possible consequences of each.

Solution	Possible Consequences of Each Solution		
A.	1.	2.	3.
B.	1.	2.	3.
C.	1.	2.	3.

CASE 2: SAFETY AND SPECIAL-NEEDS STUDENTS

Joshua is a fifth-grade student in a magnet school for children interested in math, science, and technology. He is a bright child who has been diagnosed with an attention deficit hyperactivity disorder (ADHD) and an anxiety abnormality. He is on multiple medications and sees a psychiatrist regularly due to frequent aggressive outbursts that have occurred over his 5 years in the public school setting.

Joshua has changed schools four times for various reasons and is now in a setting where, according to his mother, he has had his most success. At each previous school he was referred to the schools' assistance team by the classroom teacher for his violent out-of-control outbursts. Each time the team recommended that a change in his exceptional certification be made to address his behavior/emotional outbursts. These requests were denied based on the evaluator's requirements. For a student to have behavioral/emotional certification, all persons submitting the behavior summary must have consistent observations pertaining to the frequency, intensity, and duration of the behaviors. Joshua's mother reports that he does not exhibit these behaviors at home, and therefore the certification is denied.

On several occasions during this school year, Joshua exhibited aggressive behavior both with adults and students. Most of these situations have occurred simultaneously with a change in routine or authority. Today's outburst followed the usual pattern. Joshua's regular teacher was required to leave campus early for an after-school workshop. A teacher associate was asked to cover the classroom for the brief period of time which essentially involved dismissal.

Upon entering the room, the associate found students packing up bookbags and preparing for the daily independent, self-sustained reading program. Most students were in their seats, well aware of the routine. Joshua and two other boys were standing near the door and decided to exit the door to the picnic tables located just outside the room. The teacher associate asked the children to return to the class for the remainder of the period. Two boys responded directly; Joshua, however, stated that he was not required to follow the request because the associate was not his boss. The associate stated that he was simply requiring the same thing for all students and that Joshua had the choice to comply or go to the office. After this statement, Joshua's tone of voice and behavior began to escalate and the associate rang the office for assistance. An administrator answered the call immediately, but by the time she reached the room, Joshua was in an aggravated state which required removing the remaining students from the class to provide for their safety.

The associate went with the remaining students to the breezeway area, leaving Joshua with the principal. Additional assistance was requested from the school's student-service specialist (a psychologist) and resource teacher. Joshua's behavior continued to escalate; he ran wildly around the room, crying hysterically, and threatening to "escape" from the room no matter what the adults said. The psychologist attempted to calm Joshua down with conversation, but it became evident that this approach was not successful in solving the problem. Joshua then began jumping on desks and the bookshelves along the window area of the room. The psychologist perceived that Joshua was in what is known as the "fight or flight" mode and that he needed to secure Joshua for his own safety. He attempted to approach Joshua, who again made his way to the bookshelf area and threatened to "kill" anyone who came near him. Joshua then faced the window and struck the pane with his fist, resulting in shattering the window and cutting himself only slightly. Finally, the administrator and staff members were able to get to him and remove him safely from the ledge. After some time he calmed enough to be taken to the office area where contact was made with his mother to explain the emergency. His parent came to pick him up.

Determine the problem(s). Write and share with a colleague your own responses to each step of the model in Chapter 3, Figure 3.3 (p. 84). How can an administrator provide for the safety of all children in situations like this? What proactive measures or plans should be established to avoid future problems? Were correct procedures followed in this emergency? Is it the school's responsibility to force a change of placement via due process whenever a student's behavior is dangerous to self and others? What procedures or plans should be implemented to avoid future problems of this nature when Joshua attends middle school where change is present in the daily routine? What are some alternative plans of action for his parents to consider? Resources? What staff development seems required? For whom?

CASE 3: MENTOR OR MARTINET?

Mrs. Jones is a veteran sixth grade language arts teacher in a large middle school. She is stern with students and is a solid teacher in her content area. Teamed with her are a first-year math teacher and a second-year science/social studies teacher. Both new teachers exhibit strong knowledge in their content areas, yet they make typical rookie mistakes.

Mrs. Jones assumed the role of mentor (although she is not their assigned mentoring teacher) at the beginning of the school year. She is quite controlling during their daily planning period, particularly when it involves decisions regarding parent communication. For example, several times each month, a newsletter is sent home with each sixth-grade student to inform parents about topics taught, special assignments, and so on. Although the other two members of the team are capable of communicating effectively, Mrs. Jones insists on composing all of the newsletters. She seems to believe that novice teachers can be misleading and unclear, so she has decided to do all of the written communications to parents throughout the school year. The two novice teachers would like to be more involved with the composition and dissemination of the parent newsletter, yet they feel somewhat intimidated by Mrs. Jones and have chosen not to approach her about it.

Should the new teachers confront Mrs. Jones without involving administration? Why? Why not? How could the teachers' assigned mentors assist in this situation? How could staff development address this problem globally? How could the veteran teacher's talents be shared with the entire faculty (assuming that she has expertise in written communication)? How could the veteran teacher be approached by administrators without upsetting the team's apple cart?

For cases four and five, refer to Chapter 1, Figure 1.6 (p. 11) and establish the IS-OUGHT discrepancy conditions to help define each problem. Share your problem-framing process with a colleague and discuss differences of problem determination. Apply the steps described in Chapter 3, Figure 3.3 (p. 84).

CASE 4: SENSITIVITY AND COMMON SENSE

New staff members at Oakdale Elementary who teach autistic children are often told that they are truly part of the school family, but are often left out of certain activities. School personnel planned a special day, December 18, in the school's cafeteria. There was a contest to name the cafeteria. The students were given special instructions on good manners, and everyone at the school was asked to dress up. Participation was great. The students and staff in the autistic program participated, too.

The cafeteria was arranged like a restaurant. There were tablecloths and candles on the tables, the lights were dimmed, and a small student band played live instrumental music. There was a section for students to eat their lunch and a reserved seating section for the teachers. Once the teachers got their students through the lunch line, they were seated in the reserved seating area by the principal and the assistant principal. The administrative staff then monitored the students during lunch while the teachers were treated to a real duty-free lunch. When the autistic staff arrived and got their students through the lunch line they were not invited to sit in the reserved teacher section. Once all the regular classes had finished their lunch, the principal told the cafeteria staff to begin restoring the cafeteria to normal, even though the students and staff in the autistic program were not finished with their lunch. *No amount of technical skill will overcome insensitivity. In this case, the nonverbal communication was crucial. Although the cafeteria setting told most people that they were important, how would you have treated the "special" students and staff? Can this damage be repaired by words? How would you proceed to smooth things over?*

CASE 5: INTIMIDATION OR LEGAL ACTION?

Happy Valley School District (the county schools) has approximately 6,000 school-age children. In the school district, the multicultural mix is heavily weighted toward a white population. The African American population is 10% and the Asian population is 1%. The school district is rural and the central city in the county has its own district where the muticultural mix is closer to a 50–50 mix of white and African American students. Within the next 2 years the two systems will be consolidated due to state mandate.

Dr. Deskins, Superintendent of Happy Valley Schools, must find a replacement for Mr. George, the principal at Trails End Elementary School. Mr. George has been the principal at Trails End for over 22 years and will retire at years' end. He is the only minority administrator in the Happy Valley School District (the county). Dr. Deskins has been accused of not promoting minorities in the district, and he is keenly aware of the mounting dissatisfaction in the black community.

Mrs. Glenn is the assistant principal at Trails End. She is white and has been at Trails End for the past 4 years. She works closely with the teachers, parents, and students at Trails End, and is well liked and highly respected throughout the area.

At a recent meeting, Dr. Deskins pulled Mrs. Glenn aside. While wagging a finger in Mrs. Glenn's face he stated that he had heard about a petition that was currently being circulated by the parents and students at Trails End requesting that Mrs. Glenn be given the principalship to be vacated by Mr. George. Dr. Deskins demanded that Mrs. Glenn find the petitioners and put a stop to it. He further stated that he better not see Mrs. Glenn's name on the list of candidates for him to interview. Mrs. Glenn was shocked and hurt. She had worked hard at Trails End. Why shouldn't she apply? Mrs. Glenn left the meeting immediately. She considered talking with Dr. Williams, the Personnel Director for Happy Valley School District, but called her lawyer instead. [This scenario has been adapted from a class assignment provided by R.C. Bateman who was a student at Winthrop University.] *Personnel issues are among the most difficult problems that face a school administrator. In retrospect, what steps should each person have taken to avoid the confrontation? What steps seem reasonable now?*

WRAPPING UP

This text has tried to make education administrators—especially building-level administrators—aware of some potential minefields surrounding problems. Without skill in problem analysis, the principal runs the continuous risk of being a technician who uses only management to gain and hold public and faculty support. Problem finding, or the problem of the problem receives too little attention among many principals who are people of action, often rushing ahead to "solve" nonproblems, presented problems (other people's problems), or, worse, wasting time and effort on the wrong problem. Successful solutions come only after careful problem definition. It seems wasteful to find out after lots of hard problem-solving effort that you, and perhaps other stakeholders, may have a good solution to the wrong problem.

Experience is a major variable in separating expert and novice problem analysts. Leithwood and Steinbach (1995) found that expert principals, in contrast to novice principals, displayed greater conceptual flexibility and responsiveness, and were less influenced by mood. Achilles and Lyons (1976) conducted an experiment that showed that in professional education decisions, professional educators were able to transcend their angry, negative mood states and arrive at decisions that were essentially the same as those of their professional colleagues who registered positive and happy mood states at the time of the decisions. Leithwood and Steinbach (1995) concluded that experts avoided errors, controlled their moods, and were responsive to the opportunities of a situation. Nonexperts, at least those at the least-effective extreme, made errors, were unable to control moods, and were unresponsive to opportunities (pp. 213–214).

Although hands-on experience with real problems is the true test by fire, group analysis and discussion of cases and vignettes provide introductions to important problem-analysis processes. Each case can provide problem-finding and problem-solving practice at one level and then can be extended into an exercise in problem sharing and leadership for change (implementing the decision).

The Case Record process (see Appendix A) offers one way to document some problem-analysis activities. Attend carefully to what you, the problem analyzer, might bring into the problem situation.

Some important readings appear in the references. The Annotated Bibliography contains current sources of problem-analysis information to offer background, research results, and practical problem-analysis applications. Many of the stories told by principals in meetings are really examples of problem analysis: listen in, share a few of your experiences, and recognize that problem analysis is a great opportunity to demonstrate leadership for positive change. You, too, will benefit from practice. Start now.

Each person will have individual approaches to analyzing problem situations. Use of a structured problem-solving model helps a person remember each important step, from problem finding through evaluating the results of implementing the decision to change. Although Chapter 3, Figure 3.3 (p. 84) shows the steps inside the problem-solving process, Chapter 1, Figure 1.5 (p. 8) provides a view of the larger context of problem analysis, including the key components of problem sharing and leadership. Creativity and leadership are what good problem analysis is all about. Enjoy the challenges.

APPENDIX A

REFLECTIVENESS IN THE PROFESSIONS

by Paula F. Silver

University of Illinois, Champaign-Urbana
Apex Case Report, Vol. 1, No. 1 (October, 1984)

(The following material has been adapted. Permission to use Silver Center material was granted by K.F. Osterman, Ph.D., director of the Silver Center while it was at Hofstra University.)

Principals are very busy individuals! You know this from your own experience, and research supports the contention. There is hardly time to interpose yet another task, that of maintaining records, in the rushed life of a school administrator without sacrificing some other activities or forfeiting precious time.

If we look at other professions, however, fields such as law, medicine, and architecture, we find that practitioners do keep case records as a normal part of their hectic days. The architect's floor plan, the physician's case histories, the attorney's case briefs—all these types of case records serve vital functions for the individual professionals and for the advancement of their respective fields.

REFLECTIVE PRACTICE

One major set of advantages is associated with the individual practitioner's own continuous growth and development as a professional. This set of advantages represents the concept of *reflective practice*, a style of practice that is thoughtful, introspective, and intellectually curious. Reflective practice suggests a quest for understanding and a search for knowledge beyond what is already known about the object of practice (in this case, schools). There are at least six ways, as enumerated below, in which case record keeping contributes to reflective practice.

1. Case records help to imprint the case details in memory. Because of the disruptions and frequent interruptions of a typical day, many of the specific details of particular situations tend to slip away. Writing the details, even in brief outline form, helps us to remember exactly what happened so that we learn more systematically from experience.

2. *Case records* help to expand the search for solutions to problems. Typically, we respond intuitively to problems or issues that arise on the basis of many past experiences. Except for special projects that require detailed planning and writing, we tend to react to incidents without as much thought or as much search for the *best* response as the situation might merit.

3. *Case records* enable psychological distancing. Sometimes when people make demands, complain, challenge us, or pose problems, we feel a bit threatened by their intense feelings and tend to react ego-defensively or emotionally. The writing of case records provides a "cooling off" period and serves as a reminder that this is a professional issue, not a personal one.

4. *Case records* induce the testing of assumptions. Since the case record starts when the problem comes to our attention, the plan for a solution is like a hypothesis about what will happen as a result of our actions. We discover afterward whether the prediction was accurate. In the normal course of practice, we often do not notice when our hypotheses are *not* supported because by then we are engrossed in other ongoing events.

5. *Case records* promote systematic problem solving. Many situations we encounter in the course of day-to-day practice are amorphous and ill-defined. By calling for certain types of information (e.g., possible causes, target date, etc.) the case record helps us to impose a structure or logic or order on the events.

6. *Case records* help in meeting long-range goals. By pausing to reflect upon a range of options for action—as the professional does when writing case records—we can identify those responses that are most congruent with our broader aims. In other words, case records can help school administrators *integrate* particular incidents with important educational activities.

Expanded Knowledge

Case records advance professional knowledge. Professional knowledge production suggests the systematic and scientific accumulation of information that is oriented toward the continuous improvement of practice in the professions.

1. *Case records* enable the classification of codification of professional problems. The classifications, in turn, make it possible to organize the existing (and increasing) information so it is retrievable by practitioners as needed.

2. *Case records* reveal both unsuccessful and successful practices. School administrators often get good ideas about practice from professional publications, conferences, and colleagues. These media tend to disseminate "success stories," however, and rarely share efforts that failed. Case records provide examples of success and failure.

3. *Case records* foster the dissemination of creative ideas. Although many effective techniques and strategies are made visible in the professional journals, many ideas do not ever reach publication. The sharing of case records helps disseminate inventive solutions.

4. *Case records* facilitate joint problem solving. The availability of a written record makes it feasible for professional colleagues to bring their insights to bear on interpreting the situation and finding solutions.

5. *Case records* foster a sense of professional community. Much of the literature on professions highlights the particular *culture* and sense of community within each field. By virtue of maintaining case records, each member contributes significantly to the advancement of knowledge and practice in the field.

6. *Case records* help to merge theory and practice. By contemplating the likely causes and promising solutions to problems, professionals make their *theories-in-use* explicit.

CASE RECORD

Case Title:_____   Date:_____

Evidence of Problem:_____
_____
_____

Nature of Problem:_____
_____
_____

Possible Causes, School Based: Evidence:

_____   _____
_____   _____
_____   _____
_____   _____

Possible Causes, Self-Based: _____
_____
_____

Possible Solution: _____
_____
_____

Target Date: _____

Key Events:
Date   Event

_____|_____
_____|_____
_____|_____
_____|_____
_____|_____

Result (Date:_____):_____
_____
_____

Further Reflections: _____
_____
_____

APPENDIX B

AN EXAMPLE EMPLOYING THE PROBLEM ANALYSIS MODEL IN FIGURE 3.3

(Figure 3.3 is found at p. 84)

♦ *Case Study*: Social Mores and Religious Beliefs

Many people in the bible belt of the Blue Ridge mountains still adhere to strict moral values. Even in modern society, many of the bible belt people still believe in sexual abstinence outside of marriage, no divorce, no abortion, having children within a married Christian home, and double standards for males and females.

Scarlet McDonald was adopted by a childless couple as an infant and grew up in a strict Christian home. Miss McDonald, who is single, has been teaching for 7 years at Abletown High School. She teaches sociology and is the school sponsor for the student government association which demands much of her time, as well as after school hours. When she began teaching, Miss McDonald rapidly gained good rapport with the students. Several days a week, Scarlet McDonald's lunch period was spent talking with students who were seeking advice about friends, school, family, and so on.

New Faith, a large church located in the city limits, has a large youth group. Many members are students at Abletown High School. Miss McDonald is the youth-group advisor and is very active in other church functions. She provides a variety of activities for the youth, including guest speakers who talk about topics such as drugs, sex, marriage, and the family. Outside the school and the church, Miss McDonald has very little social life.

At the beginning of this school year, Scarlet McDonald had to miss a day or two, presumably with a stomach virus. After encouragement from peers, family, and her principal, she finally saw the doctor. After learning the diagnosis, she requested a meeting with her principal, Mr. Lavender. The principal met with her after school. Scarlet McDonald is 2 months pregnant. The baby is due at the end of May or early June. Given her background of being adopted, growing up in a strict Christian home, and being unmarried, Scarlet is torn between abortion and having the baby. After much soul searching, she decides to have the baby and to continue teaching. Mr. Lavender points out the possible repercussions as her pregnancy progresses. Scarlet has only shared her news with one other faculty member and her principal. Time passes.

Miss McDonald struggles to find cover-up clothing to hide her secret. A few rumblings are beginning to surface from students and peers about Miss McDonald gaining weight and often being sick. Mr. Lavender receives a call from a parent asking if Miss McDonald is pregnant, and if so, what does he plan to do about it? *Take the role of the principal. Use a problem-solving model (Figure 3.3, 3.4, or 3.5, pp. 84–85) and analyze this case.*

If educational administration had "pat" answers to problems and if these answers were understood by everyone, the job of principal would be a breeze! However, a facilitator/professor using the Reynolds and Silver problem-solving model (Figure 3.3), might wish to augment the problem-solving discussion with the following structure for awareness, analysis, and reflection on the problem and application of the model.

Perception is important in awareness since a person must know that she or he has a problem before it can be addressed. In the case of Scarlet McDonald's pregnancy, consider the discrepancy between right and wrong, between acceptable behavior and unacceptable behavior, and the community's acceptance and nonacceptance. The reality is that Scarlet is pregnant. The ideal situation now involves whether she can continue as a teacher in that community and be accepted or whether the principal needs to terminate Scarlet to rid the school of the "problem." One question may be what is the greatest good to be served in any of these discrepancies. As awareness, analysis, and reflection are applied, the questions change and take on new cloakings. In this sense, we may ask "What if ?" questions and reframe the situation. What if you allow Scarlet to keep her job and the pregnancy goes to term, and so on? Reframe the problem to look at situations from all angles and from other frames of reference.

The second step, seeking causes, extends awareness, analysis, and reflection. What caused this young woman to behave in this manner? Was her upbringing too strict? Were her formative years so restrictive that she really had no idea how babies were conceived? Did she meet a slick-talking person who swept her off her feet? What happened? Are there extenuating circumstances, or was Scarlet in fact a promiscuous person? What is her effectiveness as a teacher, and what will it be? What do her peers think? What do other stakeholders think?

Step three, searching for relevant information, addresses the questions suggested from a review of causes, plus any legal issues that may be involved. This a critical part of problem analysis and problem solving. In real-world practice, the more information one has, usually the better the decision. One key to an information search is the term "relevant." A principal must be able to distinguish between good and bad information. In Scarlet's case, Mr. Lavender will look to family members, staff members, church members, and perhaps some students to obtain an accurate profile of Scarlet's character and behavior. Also, the principal will need to tap the community's mood about the case and its general acceptability, both for keeping her or seeking her termination. The time factor has to be considered; how much time does Mr. Lavender have to ask questions and gather information before all of this goes too far and the decision is controlled by others and not by the principal? In reality, information search extends to all steps in the model.

In step four, after information is received and analyzed, the problem solver establishes certain goals depending on the direction being taken. Whatever the decision, goals must be addressed while considering the questions of ethics, impact, fear of failure, rejection, vulnerability, and authority to make the decision happen.

In step five the principal lays out alternatives and seeks advice and counsel in the process of beginning to share the problem and decision. Has the principal established an advisory council, preferably for this case, an ad hoc group that he can call upon for analysis, advice, and reflection in certain areas? Some questions that may need addressing are: How can we prevent this from happening again? (Optimizing.) Who are the winners and losers? (Optimizing.) How would someone else (a former mentor or principal) address this situation? What serves the greatest good or need? (Optimizing and ethics.)

In step six, selecting the preferred alternative, the principal weighs the pros and cons, perhaps applying a force-field analysis (Lewin, 1951). If Scarlet stays, what are the short-range and long-range consequences? What are the constraints? Will the greatest need be served in her staying? (Vision/discrepancy). What are the ethical considerations? Is my alternative self-serving (Am I protecting myself?) or is this choice for the betterment of the organization and of all the stakeholders?

Step seven is the plan of action. If it is well crafted and applied, what will be the benefits? Who wins and who will get credit? Who will participate in the plan? If the plan is to continue Scarlet's employment and be supportive, then who gets credit? What is the credit and how should it be distributed so everyone (stakeholders) can feel good about what they have done for this young lady, the school, and the community? On the other hand, what does the principal do if the plan is to terminate Scarlet? If this is the decision, then who takes the blame or credit? How do you address the question of winning and losing? Who makes the decisions and how? What are the ramifications of termination in a legal sense? Where do documentation and due process come into play? How much of the factual information do you or could you "leak" to protect yourself? Who needs or has to be protected? There are other issues that can be raised.

Finally, there may be some follow-up steps, and perhaps the school board should consider a policy for future similar issues. The principal should review the entire problem to consider alternative scenarios for personal growth and for evaluation of the process.

ANNOTATED BIBLIOGRAPHY

Daresh, J.C. and Playko, M.A. (1995). *Supervision As A Pro-Active Process*. 2nd ed. Prospect Hts., IL: Waveland Press, pp. 179–198. The authors offer a series of problem-solving models based on the assumption that organizational problems, even the extraordinary ones, can be identified and solutions applied. This book reinforces the basic concepts of problem finding, problem awareness, problem identification, problem causes, information search, etc. This book also provides case-study opportunities for administrators to practice without punishment at the end of each chapter.

Hallinger, P., Leithwood, K., and Murphy, J. eds (1993) *Cognitive Perspectives In Educational Leadership*. New York: Teachers College Press. The editors have selected an outstanding array of authors to present multiple perspectives on the full range of problem-based to practical applications of problem finding and problem solving. The volume includes sections on the experiences of professors teaching problem analysis, studies of expert problem solving, and examples of practical problem solving, to highlight only a few of the chapters. This volume makes a most useful collection of readings for advanced courses in problem analysis.

Kirschman, R.E. (1996). *Educational Administration: A Collection of Case Studies*. Columbus, OH: Merrill (Prentice Hall), p. vii. The author suggests that many situations for problem solving are mundane and should have a certain amount of routineness in their analysis and response. He cautions, however, that unless the practitioner uses a certain amount of planning (in thought and procedure) the practitioner might become locked into the routines to the point that carelessness might creep into the process. The author notes that inservice practice on a variety of scenarios keeps principals sharp and appropriately reflective in practice. The cases in this volume offer great opportunities for principals to study and practice problem analysis.

Leithwood, K. and Aitken, R. (1995). *Making Schools Smarter: A System for Monitoring School and District Progress.* Thousand Oaks, CA: Corwin Press. Using a real school as a springboard for developing a model of an ideal school, Leithwood and Aitken provide benchmarks and data collecting means for school administrators to use in assessing their progress. Making Schools Smarter is a handbook for collaborative assessment, strategic planning, and school and district accountability. The authors contend that leaders of a school or district must understand its entire operation in order to effect systematic change. They promote this belief in their discussions of schools as a "learning organization" that must "get smarter" to meet the changing demands of educational excellence.

Leithwood, K., and Steinbach, R. (1995). *Expert Problem Solving.* Albany, NY: State University of New York Press. Leithwood and Steinbach define "instructional leadership" and "expert administrative practices" as dependent on the formal and intuitive skills of problem solving. Their beliefs for Expert Problem Solving derive largely from the cognitive sciences perspectives as well as from practical school-based action research on how administrators find and classify problem situations as anticipated or emergency and on how their subsequent reactions correspond in priority categories. Their discussion of "transformational leader" describes the metamorphosis of change from novice to expert problem solver. Within the professional roles of teacher, principal, and superintendent, problem identification and solutions are analyzed according to levels of expertise. These contrasts in thinking processes, strategic planning, and attributable results provide the basis for the book. To support these contrasts, the book offers many tables that report affective as well as objective responses from the problem solvers. Their thinking processes plus their professional and personal values systems define "expert." Expert Problem Solving is a useful resource for educational leaders. The authors clearly

communicate their message about problem solving: a definite difference exists among school leaders in their abilities
to find and to solve problems that are hindering education's
effectiveness.

REFERENCES

Achilles, C.M. (1987, July) "Problem Solving is NOT Problem Finding." Paper at Nova Southeastern University Summer Institute: Ft. Lauderdale, FL. Nova Southeastern University.

———. (1988). "Unlocking Some Mysteries of Administration and Administrator Preparation: A Reflective Prospect." In D. Griffiths, R. Stout, and P. Forsyth (eds.). *Leaders for America's Schools*. Berkeley, CA: McCutchan, pp. 41–67.

———. (1992, January). "The Leadership Enigma is More Than Semantics." *Journal of School Leadership*, 2(1), 59–65.

———. (1990–91). "Vignette: The Balance of Trade is Scary." *National Forum of Educational Administration and Supervisors Journal*, 7(2), 31–39.

Achilles, C.M. and Lyons, D. (1976, Winter). "The Principal as Professional Decision-maker." *Educational Administration Quarterly*, XX(1), 43–53.

Achilles, C.M. and Norman, C.D. (1974, Fall). "Communication and Change in Education." *Planning and Changing*, V(3), 138–142.

Achilles, C.M. and Norris, C. (1987–88) "Vignette: Alas! A Report of a Non-Commission on Excellence in Leadership." *National Forum of Educational Administration and Supervision Journal*, 5(1), 103–107.

Allison, D. and Allison, P.A. (1993, August). "Both Ends of a Telescope: Experience and Expertise in Principal Problem Solving." *Educational Administration Quarterly*, 29(3), 302–322.

Ashbaugh, C. and Kasten, K. (1987) *Educational Leadership: Case Studies for Reflective Practice*. White Plains, NY: Longman Press.

Bailey, W.J. (1991) *School-Site Management, Applied*. Lancaster, PA: Technomic Publishing Company.

Barnard, C. (1936, March). "Mind in Everyday Affairs." (A Cyrus Fogg Brackett Lecture to the Engineering Faculty and Students, Princeton University.) In C. Barnard (ed.) (1976). *Functions of the Executive.* 2nd ed. Cambridge, MA: Harvard University Press, 307–322.

Bereiter, C. and Scardamalia, M. (1986). "Educational Relevance of the Study of Expertise." *Interchange, 17,* 10–19.

Berliner, D. (1986). "In Pursuit of the Expert Pedagogy." *Educational Researcher, 15*(7), 5–13.

Berman, P. and McLaughlin M. (1974). *Federal Programs Supporting Educational Change,* Vol. I. "A Model of Educational Change." Santa Monica, CA: Rand Corporation. See also other volumes, 1975, 1978.

Bolman, L. and Deal, T.E. (1984). *Modern Approaches to Understanding and Managing Organizations.* San Francisco: Jossey-Bass.

Brandt, R. (1988). "An Assessment of Teaching: A Conversation With Lee Shulman." *Educational Leadership, 46*(3), 42–47.

Bransford, J.D. (1993). "Who Ya Gonna Call? Thoughts About Teaching Problem-Solving." In P. Hallinger, K. Leithwood, and J. Murphy (eds.). *Cognitive Perspectives on Educational Leadership.* New York: Teachers College Press, 171–191.

Bredeson, P. (1993). "Letting Go of Outlived Professional Identities: A Study of Role Transition for Principals in Restructured Schools." *Educational Administration Quarterly, 29*(1), 34–58.

Bridges, E.M. and Hallinger, P. (1993b). *Problem-Based Learning For Administrators.* Eugene, OR: University of Oregon. ERIC Clearinghouse on Educational Management.

Campbell–Evans, G.H. (1991). "Nature and Influences of Values in Principal Decision-Making." *Alberta Journal of Educational Research, 37*(2), 167–178.

Caudill, W. (1978). "Notebook for the 1978 Walter D. Cocking Lecture." In P. Bredeson, C. Achilles, and J. Strope (eds.) (1988). *Distinguished Lectures Presented to the National Council of Professors of Educational Administration, 1976–1987.* Memphis, TN: University of Memphis (NCPEA).

Cornish, E. (1995, November/December). "Eight Steps to Innovative Problem Solving." Book review of Basadur, M. (1994). *Simplex: A Flight to Creativity.* The Creative Educational Foundation, Inc. *The Futurist, 29*(6), 49–50.

Daresh, J., and Playko, M.A. (1995). *Supervision as a Proactive Process: Concepts and Cases.* Prospect Hts., IL: Waveland Press.

Deal, T. and Peterson, K. (1994). *The Leadership Paradox.* San Francisco: Jossey–Bass.

DeBono, E. (1971). *Lateral Thinking for Management.* London: American Management Association.

Finn, J. and Achilles, C.M. (1990, Fall). "Answers and Questions About Class Size: A Statewide Experiment." *American Educational Research Journal, 27*(3), 557–577

Frederickson, N. (1984). "Implications of Cognitive Theory for Instruction in Problem Solving." *Review of Educational Research, 54,* 363–407.

Getzels, J.W. (1979). "Problem-Finding and Research in Educational Administration." In G. Immegart and W.L. Boyd (eds.). *Problem-Finding in Educational Administration.* Lexington, MA: Lexington Books, 5–22.

———. (1985, September). "Problem Finding and the Enhancement of Creativity." *NASSP Bulletin, 69*(482), 55–61.

———. (n.d.). "Problem Finding and Problem Solving." Draft. Paper prepared for the Review Team for the North Carolina School for Science and Mathematics.

Getzels, J.W. and Guba, E. (1957). "Social Behavior and the Administrative Process." *The School Review, 65,* 423–441.

Glass, G.V., Cahen, L.S., Smith, M.L., and Filby, N.N. (1982). *School Class Size: Research and Policy.* Thousand Oaks, CA: Sage.

Gorton, R.A. (1987). *School Leadership and Administrative Action.* Dubuque, IA: Wm. C. Brown.

Hallinger, P., Leithwood, K., and Murphy, J. (eds.) (1993). *Cognitive Perspectives in Educational Leadership.* New York: Teachers College Press.

Hodgkinson, H. (1985). *All One System.* Washington, DC: Institute for Educational Leadership.

———. (1991, September). "School Reform vs. Reality." *Phi Delta Kappan, 73*(1), 8–16.

———. (1992). *A Demographic Look at Tomorrow.* Washington, DC: Institute for Educational Leadership.

Holmes, C.T. and Matthews, K.M. (1984). "The Effects of Non-Promotion on Elementary and Junior High School Pupils: A Meta-Analysis." *Review of Educational Research, 54,* 225–236.

Hoover, S.G. and Achilles, C.M. (1996). *Let's Make a Deal. Collaborating on a Full-Service School With Your Community.* Thousand Oaks, CA: Corwin Press.

House, R. and Mitchell, T. (1974). "Path-Glory Theory of Leadership." *Journal of Contemporary Business, 3,* 81–97.

Hughes, L.W. and Achilles, C.M. (1971, May). "The Supervisor as a Change Agent." *Educational Leadership, 27*(8), 840–843.

Keedy, J. (1995). Draft paper on problem analysis. Personal communication.

Kirschmann, R.E. (1996). *Educational Administration: A Collection of Case Studies.* Columbus, OH: Merrill (Prentice Hall).

Kowalski, T.J. (1995). *Case Studies of Educational Administration.* 2nd ed. White Plains, NY: Longman.

Leithwood, K. (1995, March). "Cognitive Perspectives on School Leadership." *Journal of School Leadership, 5*(2), 115–135.

Leithwood, K. and Aitken, R. (1995). *Making Schools Smarter: A System for Monitoring School and District Progress.* Thousand Oaks, CA: Corwin Press.

Leithwood, K. and Stager, M. (1989). "Expertise in Principals' Problem Solving." *Educational Administration Quarterly, 25*(2), 126–161.

Leithwood, K. and Steinbach, R. (1995). *Expert Problem Solving.* Albany, NY: State University of New York Press.

Leithwood, K., Steinbach, R., and Raun, T. (1993, August). "Superintendents' Group Problem-Solving Processes." *Educational Administration Quarterly, 29*(3), 364–391.

Lewin, K. (1951). *Field Theory in Social Science*. D. Cartwright, ed. New York: Harper Brothers.

Lonsdale, R.C. (1964). "Maintaining the Organization in Dynamic Equilibrium." In D. Griffiths (ed.). *Behavioral Science in Educational Administration*, The Sixty-third Yearbook of NSSE, Part II. Chicago, IL: University of Chicago.

Lueder, D.C. (1997). *With Open Arms: Working With Hard to Reach Parents*. Lancaster, PA: Technomic.

Luft, J. (1969). *Of Human Interaction*. Palo Alto, CA: National Press Books.

McPherson, R.B., Crowson, R.L., and Pitner, N.J. (1986)." The Administrator as Problem Finder." *Managing Uncertainty: Administrative Theory and Practice in Education*. Columbus, OH: Charles E. Merill, pp. 262–286.

McWhirt, R., Reynolds, J., and Achilles, C. (1989). "You Can't Cure It If You Don't Know You Have It." *National Forum of Applied Educational Research Journal*, 2(2), 35–41.

Millerborg, A. and Hyle, A.E. (1991). "Ethics of the Law: What Drives Administrative Decisions?" *Educator's Research Report*. Norman, OK: University of Oklahoma, p. 143.

Milstein, M.M., Bobroff, B.M., and Restine, L.N. (1991). *Internship Programs in Educational Administration*. New York: Teachers College Press, pp. 224–226.

Mitchell, D.E. and Beach, S.A. (1993, May). "School Restructuring: The Superintendent's View." *Educational Administration Quarterly*, 29(2), 249–274.

Moore, P. (1990). "Writing Case Studies to Teach Article Courtesy Strategies." *Technical Writing Teacher*, 17, 18–25.

Mosteller, F. (1995, Summer/Fall). "The Tennessee Study of Class Size in the Early School Grades." *Critical Issues for Children and Youth*, 5(2), 113–127.

Murphy, J., Hallinger, P., and Mitman, A. (1983). "Problems With Research on Educational Leadership: Issues to be Addressed." *Educational Evaluation and Policy Analysis*, 5(3), 297–305.

Muse, I. (1996). *Oral and Nonverbal Expression*. Princeton, NJ: Eye on Education.

National Commission on Excellence in Educational Administration (1988). "Leaders for America's Schools." In D. Griffiths, R. Stout, and P. Forsyth (eds.). *Leaders for America's Schools: The report and papers of the National Commission on Excellence in Educational Administration.* Berkeley: McCutchan, 284–304.

National Policy Board for Educational Administration (NPBEA) (1989). *Improving the Preparation of School Administrators: An Agenda for Reform.* Charlottesville, VA: University of Virginia.

Ogawa, R.T. (1994, Fall). "The Institutional Sources of Educational Reform: The Case of School-Based Management." *American Educational Research Journal, 31*(3), 519–548.

Osterman, K. (1991, January). *Case Records. A Professional Development Strategy for School Administrators.* Hempstead, NY: Hofstra University, The Silver Center.

Peterson, K. (1986). "Vision and Problem Finding in Principals' Work: Values and Cognition in Administration." *Peabody Journal of Education, 63*(1), 87–106.

Polanyi, M. (1967). *The Tacit Dimension.* Garden City, NJ: Doubleday.

Rogers, E.M. (1962). *Diffusion of Innovations.* New York: The Free Press of Glencoe.

Rogers, E.M. and Shoemaker, F. (1983). *Communication of Innovation.* 2nd ed. New York: MacMillan.

Reynolds, J. and Silver, P. (1987). *Problem Solving.* A training module developed for the Southeastern Educational Improvement Laboratory (SEIL), Research Triangle Park, Raleigh, NC.

Savery, L. and Souter, G. (1992). "Ideal Decision-Making Styles by Deputy Principals." *Journal of Educational Administration. 30*(9), 18–25

Schmuck, R. and Schmuck, P. (1983). *Group Process in the Classroom.* Dubuque, IA: Wm. C. Brown.

Schön, D.A. (1983). *The Reflective Practitioner.* New York: Basic Books.

————. (1987). *Educating the Reflective Practitioner*. San Francisco: Jossey-Bass.

Segal, L. and Meyers, C. (1988). "Taking Aim at Problems." *Management Solutions, 33*(2), 5–8.

Senge, P. (1990). *The Fifth Discipline*. New York: Doubleday.

Shepard, L.A. and Smith, M.L. (1986). *Flunking Grades: Research and Policies on Retention*. London: Falmer.

Silver, P.F. (1984, October). *Reflectiveness in the Professions*. APEX Case Report, *1*(1). (See Appendix A, this volume.)

————. (1987). "The Center for Advancing Principalship Excellence. An Approach to Professionalizing Educational Administration." In J. Murphy and P. Hallinger (eds.). *Approaches to Administrative Training in Education*. Albany, NY: State University of New York Press, 67–82.

Smith, G.F. (1989a, August). "Defining Managerial Problems: A Framework for Prescriptive Theorizing." *Management Science, 35*(8), 963–981.

————. (1989b). "Managerial Problem Identification." *Omega, 17*(1), 27–33.

Thomson, S.D. (ed.) (1993). *Principals for Our Changing Schools: Knowledge and Skill Base*. Fairfax, VA: National Policy Board for Educational Administration (NPBEA), George Mason University.

Vail, P. (1989). *Managing As A Performing Art*. San Francisco: Jossey Bass.

Volkema, R.J. (1986). "Problem Formulation as a Purposive Activity." *Strategic Management Journal, 7*, 267–279.

Wagner, R.K. (1993). "Practical Problem-Solving." In P. Hallinger, K. Leithwood, and J. Murphy (eds.). *Cognitive Perspectives on Educational Leadership*. New York: Teachers College Press, 88–102.

Yankelovich, D. (1991). *Coming to Public Judgment: Making Democracy Work in a Complex World*. Syracuse, NY: Syracuse University Press.